CONTENTS

Introduction

ALASTAIR BURNET

It was Richard Nixon the election watcher who said, back in June, that it would be 'the longest, dullest, closest' campaign ever. He thought George Bush would win it, just.

What is probably true is that if Mr Bush loses the election he will have lost it, rather than Governor Michael Dukakis having won it.

What Mr Dukakis has done is careful and simple. He has done everything for Democratic Party unity: thus he has committed himself to living with the Revd Jesse Jackson's ego. If he continues until 8 November it means he may be assured of even better proportions of better turned-out black votes than the 85% of black men and 93% of black women voters who went for Mr Walter Mondale last time.

The other sensible thing Governor Dukakis has done is resist any temptation to worry the middle class. He forced the Democratic convention at Atlanta to vote down the policy plank, favoured by Mr Jackson's people, to put up taxes on those earning over $200,000 (£120,000) a year. Where Mr Mondale, four years ago, promised to raise taxes, Governor Dukakis promised nothing: nothing on taxes, nothing much on social welfare (beyond repeating the Democratic aim – which goes back to Harry Truman – of a comprehensive health care service), and nothing on foreign policy except to do better than the Republicans.

Mr Dukakis's policy is not to make commitments – or mistakes. He is Mr Mondale without the mistakes. That is why he is more likely to win.

In a sense, it ought to have been easy for the Republicans. At home employment is steady, prices are steady, the trade deficit is being edged down – and no one expects any hard financial decisions until January anyway. Abroad, peace has been breaking out in the Gulf and Angola and Mr Gorbachev has been biting on the bullet in Afghanistan. And Mr Bush is the heir of a highly popular President, who personified a successful election coalition, restored American self-esteem, and even took the first steps with the Soviet Union towards nuclear disarmament.

But American voters have seldom been enamoured of vice-presidents following immediately on highly popular presidents. The last one they allowed to take over was Martin Van Buren (following Andrew Jackson) in 1837. It's possible that, if the Daley machine had not stolen Illinois for Kennedy in 1960, one Richard Nixon would have had a plurality of votes then, but he would still have been short in the Electoral College. Vice-presidents (Teddy Roosevelt, Calvin Coolidge, Harry Truman, Lyndon Johnson) are best advised to take over before their predecessors' term is done.

Americans, as de Tocqueville spotted, soon get bored. They like change. They also visit the sins of popular presidents upon their heirs. On Mr Bush's head have fallen all the popular fears about the economy: so much so that, by early August, Governor Dukakis led Mr Bush by 56% to 28% as likely to do better for the middle class. So much for Mr Bush's recurrent pledge never to raise taxes. So, too, with Central America and Iran in mind, 51% of voters were 'uneasy' about Mr Bush's ability to cope in an international crisis, and only 37% were 'confident'. So much for Mr Bush's ignorance of Irangate, Colonel Oliver North, and General Noriega, the CIA and drug-running.

The week before Mr Bush went into his convention at New Orleans he was 17 points adrift. Hard work and telling the truth, he said, would put that right. And he did bounce back. Nothing wholly unusual in that. Hubert Humphrey got back almost 15 points between late September and election day in 1968; Gerald Ford got back nearly 22 points between August and election day in 1976. Of course, however well Messrs Humphrey and Ford did, they didn't win. Harry Truman in 1948 recovered from only 13% down.

Personalities do count, especially with women voters. In the race between the 'shrimp' (as Republicans call Mr Dukakis) and the 'wimp' (as Democrats call Mr Bush), Mr Bush is badly adrift with the women. Then there's the political alliances across the continent. In FDR's day it was the alliance of the machine-controlled cities, the farmers and the South that won him four in a row. The Eisenhower years saw the Republicans stifling the cities with the suburbs and detaching the farmers. The Goldwater campaign in 1964, though overwhelmed by LBJ, finally detached the old South.

The key to the Nixon–Reagan years (1969–74 and 1981–8), in which the Republicans made themselves into the natural presidential majority, depended on putting the South, the farm states and the West (both candidates were California's favourite sons) together, and counter the poor, black, elderly city Democrats with the right-of-centre predilections of the ethnics (German-

American, Polish-American, Italian-American, even Jewish-American voters) whenever the Democrats selected left-wing candidates like Humphrey, McGovern and Mondale.

This is the Republican alliance that President Reagan has left behind him. The problem for Mr Bush's managers is that Mr Reagan was exceptionally good at putting it together. Thus, in 1984, he took 55% of the Catholic vote, 53% of the blue-collar vote, 45% of union households, 34% of Democrats who had voted for Senator Gary Hart in the primaries, and even 33% of Hispanics. In all these categories – the decisive crossover voters – Mr Bush has been lagging behind.

Governor Dukakis, naturally, has studied the last two successful Democrats in close elections: Kennedy in 1960, Carter in 1976. Artlessly, he picked the conservative Senator Lloyd Bentsen of Texas to run with him as Kennedy picked Johnson. Mr Bentsen may not bring in too much of the South (Kennedy–Johnson took Georgia, both Carolinas, Louisiana, half Alabama) but he will be potent in a bankrupt Texas (as Texas is) and as both Governor Dukakis and he are fluent in Spanish, there's New Mexico and southern California to hope for. Though probably not anti-Castro Florida.

In this, the American economy has helped the Democrats. It is no longer as true as it was that the Republicans have the growing, booming, high-tech Sun Belt and the Democrats are left with the rusty old North-East. Tell that to the oilmen in Houston (where Mr Bush still keeps a hotel room) or the bankers in Dallas–Fort Worth. Massachusetts's unemployment has been below the national average for years now; the old mill towns are high-tech places.

Governor Dukakis naturally claims the credit. It's a nice question whether that's right or whether the credit should really go to Mr Ed King, the man who beat him in 1978, or even to the Reagan administration's defence spending which put profits into every plant along the old Route 128. When Governor Dukakis points to his record it's also a nice question if he does know how to balance a budget.

The Dukakis campaign will probably sweep the North-East anyway, just as Mr Bush should sweep the South. Parts of Kentucky and Tennessee usually declare early and will give pointers, but the first sign of the real test in the Great Lakes states will come in Ohio (which went to Carter by 11,118 votes in 1976, to Truman by 7,107 in 1948). The farmers, and the farming industries, will be influenced by the administration's handling of the drought and Common Market competition. Oklahoma is the one state which hasn't had a drought, but the harvest isn't shared by the oilmen.

And there is the great enigma, California (47 electoral votes). In the ten elections since the war the Republicans have had a Californian on their ticket eight times (Earl Warren, Richard Nixon, Ronald Reagan), and they've taken the state eight times. Although California is still voting when the East Coast results are announced, it hasn't mattered in the outcome since 1916, when Woodrow Wilson took it from Hughes by just 3,420 and went on to the war against Germany, the Versailles peace and failure over the League of Nations on those votes. California was only worth 13 electoral votes then, like North Carolina today, but it was decisive.

Whatever Mr Bush's hopes of Senator Dan Quayle as his running mate, not least in the Midwest, the Senator is not a Californian – even if he has semi-Hollywood looks.

Who cares about the election? Well, Mr Gorbachev, Mrs Thatcher (who is to meet the winner in late November), every other head of government, the Japanese (who fear Senator Bentsen's protectionism – they'd heard of him long before they heard of Governor Dukakis), every leader of every opposition (have the Democrats at last found the answer to Reaganism/Thatcherism?), and everyone who sells to or buys from, or whose hopes and fears are touched by, America. It is still the most important election in the world. And it could be the longest, dullest and closest for quite a time.

And the one place in all America that has always voted for the winner since 1896 is Crook County, Oregon. (Palo Alto, Iowa, went crook in 1984, voting for Mondale.) Crook's got more trees than people, but someone there seems to know more than we know.

CHAPTER ONE
The Reagan Years –
1981-1988

DOMESTIC ASSESSMENT
Robert Waller
Director of Social and Political Research, the Harris
Research Centre

It is by now quite clear that in the USA, as in Britain, the 1980s (like the 1950s), will be seen as a decade dominated by right-wing politics and conservative governments. The rather glum tone of the intellectuals' recent reminiscences about 1968 suggest that in both countries the era of challenge by idealistic youth has passed on; indeed President Reagan has had no more enthusiastic band of admirers than first-time voters and even 'pre-voters'.

For eight years Mr Reagan and Mrs Thatcher have stood together warmly, shoulder to shoulder, casting themselves as leaders of the 'free world', opponents of socialism and of the advance of the frontiers of the state. Each has enjoyed overwhelming landslide re-election. As the President retires, the Prime Minister forges on in her third term with seemingly undiminished determination and energy. However, Ronald Reagan's achievement should not be underestimated, for all the querulous carping of his critics. If indeed the remarkably diverse US in the 1980s could be described as 'Reagan's America', as much as we are 'Thatcher's Britain', that would be to make an even greater claim to achievement.

In far too many ways Ronald Reagan's reputation in Britain has been distorted by the spitting image he has attracted on our television. As a result his popularity within the States has not been understood. How could someone portrayed as a septuagenarian and amnesiac buffoon of an ex-movie actor be respected at home or abroad? Yet respected and popular he has remained within his own country, particularly among the young, who are so influenced by television. Among 13–17-year-olds asked who they would be more likely to vote for when they were old enough, the Republicans reversed a 12% lead for the Democrats in 1982, drawing level in 1983 and taking a lead which reached 9% in 1984 and 19% (1985), 18% (1986), and 14% (1987).

Faith in Reagan's Presidency spread throughout the US population in the 1980s. According to one benchmark, those 'trusting the Government in Washington to do what is right all or most of the time', this Republican anti-statist managed to boost belief in the federal centre from the low ebb inherited from an interventionist Democrat, Jimmy Carter. In November 1980 this pollsters' index of faith in central government stood at just 26%; by November 1982, mid-way through Reagan's first term, it reached 34%. On Reagan's re-election it stood at 45%, as measured both by CBS and by the University of Michigan's National Election Study. According to this criterion 'trust' has remained solidly in the 'forties' ever since.

The scope of Reagan's re-election triumph in 1984 should not be underestimated. He won 49 states, losing only one, Walter Mondale's own Minnesota (in 1980 he had conceded only six states to Carter). He was not challenged by any other Republicans in the primaries, and in the presidental election he polled 59%, which compared with a mere 48% and 41% achieved by the two most recent previous incumbents who ran (unsuccessfully) for re-election, Gerald Ford and Jimmy Carter. It is true that Reagan benefited from Walter Mondale's identification with a 'rainbow coalition' of minorities rather than with the centre ground of 'middle America'. He undoubtedly tapped both the well-timed economic recovery in the States in early 1984, and also the 'ratchet' effect of patriotism generated by the Los Angeles Olympic Games that summer. Underlying these more transient factors, though, were deeper optimistic trends.

One crucial indicator on both sides of the Atlantic is the response to the question, 'Which party will do a better job of keeping the country prosperous?' The Republicans retained a Gallup poll lead in this respect from 1980 right up to 1988, with the exception of the period of Reagan's mid-first-term slump of 1982–3. Personal optimism was also the hallmark of the Reagan years. More than 50% of Americans expected to be better off financially in a year's time from 1984 right through to 1988; throughout this period, less than 20% expected to be worse off. Nor was this perception far from true. The American economy has created 11 million new jobs since 1978. Inflation, which threatened to pass 20% at the beginning of the decade, faded almost to nothing – to be replaced as the leading issue of concern by non-economic matters, such as drugs and crime.

It is scarcely surprising, given the growth of the American economy in the 1980s, after its stagnation in the 1970s, that the President's approval ratings remained high: consistently more than 50% of Americans polled favoured the way he was handling his job from 1981 right through to 1987 (with a slight slump into the forties in 1982).

It is also worth remembering that in the 1980s, despite alarms over the Middle East and the Caribbean spheres, the US has remained a nation at peace. There may have been Iran, and Grenada – but no Korea, no Vietnam; and no draft (to which Reagan has been strongly opposed) and no disaffected generation risking all on battlefields or in jungles or demonstrating against involvement. Americans, in general, have been left to exercise their enterprise, to make money; and many of them have succeeded in doing just that.

Like Mrs Thatcher, Ronald Reagan gave Americans the impression that he was on top of his job – a distinct contrast to his harassed predecessor, Jimmy Carter. His laid-back – some would say lazy – style was widely seen as a sign of relaxed control rather than of indolence or incompetence. Before 'Irangate', the occasional excursions into foreign policy (such as the invasion of Grenada) were interpreted as the eagle stretching its wings, rather than as the actions of a hectoring bully.

It is not just the American reverence for their President – Head of State rather than a mere politician – which would lead most of his citizens to regard the Spitting Image portrayal of Ronald Reagan as offensive and ludicrous. For many of them, he 'did the business', the budget deficit being more than outweighed by the reduction in unemployment and inflation, the slips and gaffes outweighed by the calm fireside manner which is far from wholly scripted.

Yet there is another side of American politics in the 1980s which must distinguish Reagan's regime from Margaret Thatcher's. No one should mistake a Reagan dominance for a Republican dominance – and it is this which threatens George Bush's succession to his Number One's job. The US party system is infinitely more complex than our own. Reagan is not the leader of the Republican Party, nor will Bush be, nor Dukakis of the Democrats. That there is no such position as Party Leader demonstrates that 'Republican' and 'Democrat' are merely labels adopted by a wide variety of politicians for a plethora of reasons which strongly depend on which state one comes from. The most 'liberal' politicians are usually Democrats; but so may be the most 'conservative', particularly in the Deep South, where people still 'vote as they shot' (against the Northerners under the Republican Lincoln in the Civil War). Presidential elections can create the illusion of a two-party system, but local politics in this vast country still repay the closest of attention.

It is largely through the amalgamation of the numerous local political contests – and the many cleavages around which the parties divide, and the true independence of many elected politicians – that Congress has not been under Reagan's control even in 'his' 1980s. It is true of course that there are congressional elections every two years, so that half of them take place in the president's potentially unpopular 'mid-term'. Yet the reasons for the failures of the presidential party in Washington DC cannot be explained just by 'mid-term blues'. The Senate *was* captured by Republicans in 1980 on Reagan's coat-tails, after twenty years of Democratic control; yet it was lost again in 1986, even while the President's own ratings remained high. The House has not been even within shouting distance of a Republican majority for decades. In November 1986, 258 Democrats were elected and only 177 Republicans. In theory – and to a large extent in practice – this split between control of the Legislature and the Executive could lead to the effective blocking of presidential initiatives (such as financial support for the Contras in Nicaragua). Reagan could have had few more formidable opponents than the Democratic Speaker of the House of Representatives until 1986, Tip O'Neill, or his successors Jim Wright (Majority Leader) and Thomas Foley (Majority Whip). The Democratic majority in the lower house is now entrenched, and they are unlikely to lose the Senate (now 54–46 in their favour) again in the foreseeable future, whoever wins the 1988 presidential race.

However, this Democratic majority is not a liberal majority, nor would it necessarily be a majority for Dukakis. The art of congressional politics is coalition-building, across parties, around particular issues, or on more general ideological lines. The most frequent and likely coalition tends to be a little to the right of centre, based on mainstream Republicans and southern Democrats. This reflects the national political temper.

After all, an ABC News survey at the middle of this decade found that twice as many Americans (43%) considered themselves to be conservative as liberal (21%), with the remaining 36% nominating themselves as 'moderate'. As in Britain, the electorate remains predominantly centrist, for all the activism of the ideologues of left and right over the past couple of decades.

Nor should we ignore the geographical variation in response in the US to Reagan's presidency. There are the traditional – even historical – regional allegiances: the Deep South to 'moral' conservatism, by whichever party it is purveyed; the individualist 'frontier' anti-welfarism of the West and the Rocky Mountains; the idealism of northern California and the materialism of southern California; the competitive pragmatism of farmers and manufacturers in the Midwest; and the stark ethnic awareness and divisions of the North-East, including New England.

In the 1980s, however, the explanation of political choice and behaviour came also to rely on and be defined by economic attributes. Thus there was discerned a 'Sun Belt', to which major companies preferred to relocate, creating boom cities in south-western states like Utah (Salt Lake City), Arizona (Phoenix) and New Mexico (Albuquerque). There was also a 'Rust Belt', characterized by declining heavy industries and more general blight, centred on midwestern states like Michigan and Ohio, the old 'foundry' of America. The so-called 'Oil Patch' (Texas, Louisiana, Oklahoma) passed through boom and slump dependent on commodity prices. The rapid modernization of the southern economy attracted back many blacks who had left for northern cities in the previous half-century. New England, especially Massachusetts, recovered from high unemployment in the early 1980s to a 'high-techology'-led growth for which, even within the Reagan years, Governor Michael Dukakis has received much credit.

The regional variations encapsulate only to some extent the racial politics of this divided nation. Wherever they live, black Americans can be expected to register and to turn out to vote less enthusiastically than most other ethnic groups. This tends to devalue their almost totally solid support for Democratic candidates. The concentration of blacks in inner-city areas guaranteed over twenty seats for black congressmen in the House of Representatives throughout the 1980s, but sheer numbers denied the minority any Senate seats or a realistic possibility of the presidency or vice-presidency.

A more rapidly growing ethnic group, commonly known as Hispanic or Spanish-speaking, is in fact made up of at least four distinct strands: the Puerto Ricans, mainly settled in New York City; the Chicanos, or emigrants from Mexico, who crossed the border to southern California and Texas; the long-established Spanish-speakers of New Mexico and other parts of the South-West; and the much more conservative Cubans, fleeing as exiles from Castro's Communist regime, who have pushed Florida to the right in the last decade or so. The political preferences of these groups are varied. Reagan has had few Hispanic opponents in Miami, few supporters in New York City. The study of the Hispanic vote in the States presents a salutary warning against ethnic stereotyping in politics.

One other 'demographic' variation in support which is of interest is the 'gender gap' in response to Ronald Reagan's politics, which have been more popular among men than women. This is a new phenomenon in the 1980s (traditionally, as in Britain, women were more conservative than men). This change may largely be put down to the administration's 'macho' foreign policy, which succeeded in beating the drum without endangering the lives of many American men. At the very end of his presidency, Reagan's chances of passing on his mantle to his deputy still seem threatened by the gender gap, as polls consistently have showed.

According to Harris in early June 1988, there was a lead of 14% for Michael Dukakis among women, while George Bush was the preferred candidate among men by 5%.

The question arises, especially given the weakness of the American party system, as to whether Reagan can hand over to a Republican successor. Much of the success he enjoyed in the central years of his period of office was personal in nature. It should be noted that the Conservative Party would not look so strong or so invincible here were Mrs Thatcher not to be leader, but the medium-term prospect for right-wing government in Britain into the 1990s seems healthier than in the US. Reagan's era seems to be ending on a down-note as yet to afflict British Conservatives. The 'Irangate' crisis cast doubt on the wisdom and judgment of his government's foreign policy in a crucial and unstable area. The problems surrounding the departure of Attorney-General Edwin Meese cast doubt (not for the first time) on Reagan's ability to select appropriate senior advisers and to control them. Nor does the economy itself appear so trouble-free that the Republican succession can be assured without an incumbent president.

Michael Dukakis has had a successful time since 1982, when he recovered the governorship of the Commonwealth of Massachusetts. He also has 'presided' over a booming economy, with an air of more active managerialism than the Reagan administration has. What is more, his star has waxed, not waned, over the past twelve months. A Harris poll conducted in early summer 1988 suggested that on the vital issue of who might keep the United States prosperous, Bush and Dukakis were tied at 44%. 1988, unlike any election since 1976, has all the hallmarks of a close-run thing. A Reagan Republican 1980s has a very fair chance of being succeeded by a Dukakis Democratic 1990s.

FOREIGN POLICY ASSESSMENT
Jon Snow
ITN Diplomatic Editor

'America is back, standing tall' – this, in the 1984 election, was one of the key catchphrases with which Ronald Reagan campaigned his way across the United States to win the landslide vote that put him into the White House for a second term.

If his foreign policy objective had merely been to make America feel good about herself, then in large measure he succeeded. Certainly he inherited from Jimmy Carter an American morale brought low by the 444-day-old hostage crisis with Iran. Fifty-two American diplomats had been seized by fundamentalist Islamic students in Tehran; from the moment, in November 1983, when the hostages were taken, Carter's administration had seemed to become hostage itself to the developing chaos inside Iran. From the outset Reagan determined to restore confidence and strength to America's international profile. On the very day of his inauguration, 20 January 1981, the hostages were flown to freedom, handing him a handsome propaganda coup upon which to build his America 'standing tall'.

There were two other planks of foreign policy upon which he consistently campaigned, both before he became president and during his successful bid for re-election. They were inter-related: the first centred upon rolling back what he perceived to be an appeasing posture of detente with the Soviet Union; the second involved 'holding the line' in America's 'backyard' against what he described as the 'tide' of communism threatening America's own southern borders.

In and around these core themes Reagan found himself sanctioning the shelling of the Lebanon with the battleship *New Jersey*; losing 241 marines to a car bomb in Beirut; invading the tiny Caribbean island of Grenada; mining the Nicaraguan port of Corinto; bombing Colonel Gadaffi's tented home in the Libyan capital of Tripoli; and putting his arm round the shoulder of his Soviet counterpart in Red Square. By the closing months of his administration, polls indicated that, in general, Americans did 'feel better' about the United States than at the equivalent time in the Carter years; but many American critics charged that Reagan's pursuit of strength had been fraught with risks and that, in the end, he had been the beneficiary of one of the greatest strokes of good fortune to befall any American president – the coming to power of Mikhail Gorbachev in the Soviet Union.

Mrs Nancy Reagan is often credited with having regularly considered the position her husband might eventually occupy in the history books. That position may well eventually depend upon the success or otherwise of his foreign policy; upon the extent to which he rebuilt America's confidence in herself; upon his handling of East–West relations and arms control; and upon the extent to which he succeeded in his goals in America's backyard.

It was not only in Iran that American confidence had flagged under Carter. Many Republicans and not a few Democrats reckoned things had been going badly wrong for the United States in Central America too. President Carter had determined that human rights considerations should play a paramount role in deciding American policy in other countries. The corrupt and brutal Somoza dictatorship in Nicaragua had proved too much for the Carter administration's continued support. After the American television news correspondent, Bill Stewart, was killed in cold blood in front of his own camera by a Nicaraguan national guardsman, Carter blocked all further aid to the beleaguered regime, and Somoza fell. Initially Carter sent aid, but as the success of the Nicaraguan leftist Sandinistas began to infect neighbouring countries with revolutionary fervour, Carter began to panic. El Salvador had had its US military aid frozen following the murder of Archbishop Romero and the killings of thousands of civilians by right-wing death squads. Just before leaving the presidency, Carter restored the aid.

Upon entering the White House, Mr Reagan perceived a bubbling cauldron of revolutionary trouble threatening US interests in the region, and US borders further north. He immediately increased military aid to El Salvador, and launched a covert war designed to overthrow the Sandinistas in Nicaragua. Neither policy attracted widespread support domestically in America, and the Nicaraguan policy in particular was a source of endless friction between the White House and Capitol Hill. Although Reagan by the end appeared to have prevented El Salvador from slipping into the hands of a revolutionary movement as ill-disposed to Washington as the neighbouring Sandinistas, by 1988 the right-wing death squads were active again, picking off prominent civilians. And in the closing days of the Reagan administration, the Sandinistas were battered but still very much in command in Managua despite a US economic embargo and a multi-million-dollar covert war effort against them.

Further south, the drug-running Noriega regime in Panama continued in power, with American connivance. Only the election year of 1988 and rumour trails that ran dangerously close to the Vice-President's office provoked any keenness to remove Noriega.

It is questionable whether any of Reagan's enterprises in Central America earned him many 'brownie points' at home. They certainly made him popular with the once vital, once influential conservative circles that brought him to the forefront of American politics in the first place. But within the wider electorate, polls suggested that the majority was not much impressed. Indeed, amongst liberals the involvement in Central America raised the spectre of Vietnam that has haunted the United States for two decades.

Reagan's policies in the Middle East and the Gulf raised the same spectre. His attempt to act as policeman in the disintegrating state of Lebanon ended disastrously in October 1983 with the killing of 241 marines in a car-bomb blast at their headquarters at Beirut International Airport. Peacekeeping in the Gulf, in an effort to apply pressure upon Iran and to ensure the free passage of shipping, was costly both in naval ships and in lives, most specifically when, on 17 May 1987, the guided-missile destroyer *Stark* was hit by an Iraqi missile, killing 37 American seamen. Even so this policing endeavour proved more popular at home, not least because the seizing of American hostages in Tehran back in 1979 had ensured that Iran remained the 'great enemy'. So much so that when in July 1988 the American warship *Vincennes* accidentally shot down an Iranian airbus killing the nearly three hundred passengers and crew aboard, there was no sense of outrage back in America and, despite promises of compensation, little sign of contrition.

Over the years, like Carter before him, Reagan became dogged by a hostage crisis. But the hostages were taken over a number of years, and were held, only indirectly under Iranian control, in Lebanon. Although Reagan acted tough, his administration struck covert deals involving the supply of tons of military material in exchange for hostages and money for the war effort in Central America. What became known as the Iran–Contra affair threatened to become one element of Reagan's rule that the history books would not easily ignore. Publicly, Reagan had set his face against any kind of 'deal' to win the freedom of more than a dozen US hostages held by pro-Iranian factions in Beirut. But during 1984 and 1985 his aides were secretly negotiating with the authorities in Tehran. The essence of the deal they struck involved sending shipments of weapons to Iran in return for money paid into Swiss bank accounts. These in turn provided funds for the White House's covert 'Contra' war against Nicaragua. The affair was blown before it was ever able to deliver the hostages' freedom.

Beyond the continuing hostage crisis and the policing of the Gulf, Reagan, unlike Carter, showed little interest in taking new initiatives to resolve the core Arab–Israeli dispute in the Middle East. Secretary of State George Shultz visited the region less frequently than most of his predecessors, and although the West and the Soviets generally warmed to the idea of an international conference to look at the problem, Reagan appeared unwilling to use his very considerable influence to try to persuade the reluctant and conservative Israeli Prime Minister Yitzhak Shamir to agree to such a conference.

Beyond East-West negotiations - to which we shall turn in a moment - there were few outright foreign policy successes. The removal of the Philippine dictator and erstwhile US friend, Ferdinand Marcos, from office and his replacement by Corazon Aquino was in large measure due to some nifty behind-the-scenes footwork by American diplomats. However, at the end of his administration there are few who would be rash enough to predict that American policy in the Philippines, and the US bases there around which so much turns, are at all secure. But persuading South Korea's President Chun Doo Hwan to agree to constitutional changes which led not only to his demise but to the creation of a civilian government was no small achievement.

These successes have to be balanced with other failures such as Reagan's policy of 'constructive engagement' with South Africa. No American president has presided during so powerful a change of heart as that which the business community had on South Africa. There was a wholesale withdrawal of investment by American companies and institutions.

Few of Reagan's foreign policy initiatives are likely to place him very positively in the pages of history. The invasion of the diminutive island of Grenada was regarded by those about him as a coup - coming on the heels of the massive loss of service personnel in the Beirut marine barracks bombing. Subsequent congressional investigation suggested, however, that the Grenada operation had been fraught with mistakes, including several incidents in which US personnel killed their own people by mistake. The bomb runs against Libya's Colonel Gadaffi were not much more successful and provoked considerable dissent within the Western alliance. Yet both in Grenada and in Libya, Reagan's preparedness and capacity to strike appealed to many in the US. Opinion polls at the time found surges in his popularity after both events. Americans appeared less interested in the specifics of either event, but seemed relieved that strong decisive action had been taken in both. Those who criticized at such times tended to be ridiculed as somehow unpatriotic. In both practical and diplomatic terms neither the invasion of Grenada nor the bombing of Libya was a success, but both events lent themselves well to the sense that 'America is back'.

Much of America's new strength under Reagan was expressed in his willingness to build US stockpiles, weapons systems and manpower to a level unprecedented in American peacetime history. In October 1981 the Reagan administration announced a

$180 billion across-the-board bolstering of US nuclear forces. It was the backbone of Reagan's drive to revive American morale and raise the US profile in the world. Although the Pentagon never got what it demanded in budget terms, Reagan's defence budgets were spectacular in scale, rising from $221.6 billion in 1982 to an estimated $290.8 billion in 1988.

It was against this backdrop that Reagan sought to negotiate on arms control with the Soviets. Moscow was not alone in its fear of what the early days of the Reagan administration might herald. There were many in the Western alliance who felt decidedly uncomfortable at some of what was coming out of the White House. Reagan himself called the Soviet Union the 'evil empire', and said Russians were 'liars and cheats'. His senior National Security Council military advisor, Major-General Robert L. Schweitzer, caused a furore when he contended there was a 'drift towards war'. He also said that the Soviets were 'going to strike'.

In the early Reagan years the policy was not only to rebuild America's physical strength but also to seize the moral high ground. The Soviet invasion of Afghanistan in late 1979 had already left the USSR in a poor light in terms of international public relations. 1 September 1983 handed Reagan a propaganda weapon that took Soviet–American relations to their lowest point in a decade or more. The Soviets shot down a Korean passenger jet, killing all 269 people aboard, after it had entered Soviet airspace illegally. The East–West arms control dialogue, which had anyway taken a nose-dive from the heady days of Carter's SALT 2 negotiations, dived still further and all negotiations were broken off. Whilst the Kremlin old guard died year by year, the Reagan administration talked loudly of the Soviet menace. The Soviets deployed their SS20 missiles along their European frontiers; the Americans followed suit with their Cruise and Pershing missiles. The tension continued to rise.

Then in March 1985, Mikhail Gorbachev took over in the Kremlin, at the age of 54. He was the fourth Soviet leader in three years, and the youngest member of the Politburo. By November of the same year Reagan and he were sitting down in Geneva for the first superpower summit in six years.

The atmosphere at that summit was extraordinary. The anthropological fascination of seeing the most outspoken anti-Soviet ever to occupy the White House openly discussing the reduction of tension between the two great power blocs took some getting used to. For the first time in nearly two years each side sent negotiators to Geneva to work at a deal to reduce medium-range nuclear weapons whilst at the same time tackling issues of human rights, the resolution of regional conflicts, and the solution of the wider nuclear issues.

Frustrated by the lack of progress, in October 1986 Gorbachev got Reagan to agree that they would meet again in Reykjavik. It was another bizarre event – a meeting at which Gorbachev very nearly persuaded Reagan to sign a deal removing *all* nuclear weapons from the face of the earth by the year 2000. That Reagan came so close to agreeing to such a deal caused considerable misgivings amongst the Western allies – not least Mrs Thatcher who within weeks was re-affirming her belief that she could not foresee the nuclear weapons that had kept the peace for 40 years being removed in her lifetime.

At the Washington summit in 1987, and by the Moscow summit in 1988, the INF or medium-range nuclear missile ban had been concluded, and in Red Square Reagan threw his arm around Gorbachev's shoulders ... embracing the man who had once been the leader of the 'evil empire', in command of the 'liars and cheats'.

After eight years in the White House Reagan still clung to his dream of an anti-nuclear-missile shield above the earth that would render inter-continental missiles useless. To many scientists world-wide, it was a pipe dream. But the experience of office seemed to have turned Reagan into a pragmatist. By the end he was prepared to negotiate where once he had steadfastly refused. Although the strategic arms treaty has eluded him, he is likely to have set the tone for arms control for many years of East–West relations to come.

Whatever the history books eventually make of the Reagan years, he himself has explained the transformation of life with Moscow as having come about because America was negotiating from strength. He has argued that the success of the whole arms control endeavour is testimony to the reality that 'America *is* back' *and* 'standing tall'.

ECONOMIC ASSESSMENT
Derek Scott
City economist

President Reagan's eight years of office have been marked by two opposing trends in economic fortunes: the deepest recession in the US since the 1930s and the strongest recovery in post-war history. A judgment of any president has to take account of the times in which policies are implemented – some periods of history are economically less turbulent than others – but those most clearly associated with President Reagan, the so-called 'Reaganomics', featured more obviously in the recovery than in the recession of 1981–2. Although the Reagan administration cannot dissociate itself from the key policies operated by the Federal Reserve (FED), for which there seemed no practical alternative, these had been initiated whilst Jimmy Carter was still president.

Since 1982, the application of 'Reaganomics' has resulted in a rapid increase in living standards, more jobs and a marked decline in the unemployment rate, to its lowest level since 1974. Productivity growth, whilst lower than that achieved during the early post-war years, is still a substantial improvement over the period between the two oil shocks of the early 1970s and 1980s. Most importantly, there has been a distinct improvement in the trade-off between growth and inflation. However, the other side of this rosy picture shows large fiscal deficits, sharp fluctuations of the dollar exchange rate, and the build-up of current account deficits. The US is a net debtor for the first time since 1914.

Reagan's 1980 presidential victory and the accompanying Republican capture of the Senate were as clear a mandate for conservative philosophy and policy as there has been in the post-war US. The main features of economic policy were clear enough.

The most obvious plank of the Reagan platform was tax cuts. This represented an important shift from the traditional emphasis on 'Keynesian' demand management to supply-side economics. Such economic policies work on the assumption that people will work harder, save more and increase investments if personal taxation is reduced. The administration never adopted the extreme supply-side view that tax cuts could lead to revenue increases. However, these cuts were expected to be paid for by a combination of increased saving and budget cuts, thus encouraging additional capital spending by the private sector.

A second and closely associated aim was the desire to reduce the growth of federal spending, accompanied by a commitment to a balanced budget. Philosophically this can be seen as a traditional conservative desire to reduce the size and role of government.

From an economic point of view, it was argued that a reduction in the call on savings from the public sector would release funds into private, productive channels.

Thirdly, the rate of inflation was seen as a purely monetary phenomenon. The outlines of monetary policy had been set in motion by the FED before the new administration took office. Some of the monetarist economists within the administration believed that there could be a rapid transmission of monetary restraint into a lower rate of inflation, with a corresponding, smaller impact on unemployment. They were wrong. Interest rates remained high by historical standards and the recession deepened. The FED eased policy from June 1982–May 1983. Latterly, the actions of the FED aimed at sustaining growth so long as inflation appeared to be under control.

The most distinctive features of the Reagan years are to be seen in fiscal policy. At its core were two pieces of legislation: the Economic Recovery Tax Act of August 1981 and the Tax Reform Act of December 1986.

On assuming office, the administration proposed three successive annual cuts of 10% in personal income tax rates, beginning on 1 July 1981. Although the first of these was reduced to 5% and postponed for three months, taxpayers further benefited when Congress added provisions for annual indexation of personal income tax brackets and allowances to cover the rise in consumer prices from the beginning of 1985. In addition to personal income tax cuts the administration put forward standardized, simplified and increased business depreciation allowances.

The 1981 Act was successful in cutting taxes but did nothing to remove the many distortions in the tax system itself. The Tax Reform Act of 1986 specifically addressed the issue by focusing on tax equity: the attempt to ensure that any two people with the same income (from whatever source) would be paying the same amount of tax. The inevitable compromises had to be made with Congress, but it was a bold attempt to reform a system in which tax benefits of little use to the economy were often chosen instead of more soundly based investments.

If reducing personal taxation generally encourages people to work harder and save more, then those who react accordingly will obviously be well rewarded. However, the equation is rather more complex. It is a balance between choosing to work in time formerly spent at leisure because it now pays to do so (the substitution effects) and reducing the need to work long hours because real income has increased for a given amount of effort (the income effects). In practice individuals are not always free to make such choices and the effects of taxation on the supply of labour and on saving are not at all easy to calculate. The effects of tax reform on capital expenditure seem to have been more marked than on personal savings, which declined to an all-time low. This was contrary to the views of some of the President's advisers who thought the tax reforms would encourage personal savings.

Cuts in taxation were one side of the administration's coin. The other was cutting public expenditure. The two were integral parts of the plan to balance the federal budget in 1984. However, although the administration wanted to cut total public spending it also wanted to increase defence expenditure. This was programmed to rise at an annual rate of 8% in real terms between 1981 and 1987, compared with less than 2% between 1975 and 1981. The defence build-up began quickly but cuts in non-defence expenditure fell well short of the administration's target: the government was looking particularly for big savings on social security. Following the tax cuts, the result was inevitable: far from declining, the federal deficit soared.

The impasse was a political failure in the admittedly protracted budgetary process in the US. The dispute touched key political sensitivities: defence policy, the role of incentives, income distribution through social security, other public expenditure and direct taxation, and the role and influence of government itself. Both sides acknowledged the serious economic consequences of the constitutional deadlock. The soaring deficits would either absorb all personal savings within a few years, transfer much of the burden of financing these deficits to overseas countries, or force the FED into financing the deficits with the inevitable inflationary results. It was this realization, as the deficit doubled to $200 billion during an economic recovery which should have reduced it, that forced the passage of the Gramm–Rudman–Hollings Act. This imposed the requirement to adhere to a designated deficit target. In 1987 the deficit was $150 billion and a similar figure is expected for 1988.

Thus from the very beginning, the balance of policy was not that which the authors of the programme had envisaged. But it is the one which has shaped the distinctive characteristics of economic policy throughout the Reagan years and set the agenda for his successor. One of the effects was high interest rates, and a surge in the dollar. The speed and extent of this rise undermined the trading competitiveness of the US and the trade gap widened.

Arguably there was no simple relationship between the strength of the dollar up to 1985, the high real interest rates, and the policy mix of large federal deficits and monetary policy. The attractiveness of both US corporate and dollar assets was supported by the good performance of the US economy in terms of growth and inflation after 1982. Overseas holdings of corporate shares more than doubled as did direct investment, attracted by the enhanced investment opportunities in the US. However, other commentators argue that the shift in fiscal policy, both in the US and abroad, together with the period of tightened monetary policy can explain up to two-thirds of the rise in the dollar and the widening external deficit.

What is clear is that foreign exchange markets shifted very swiftly. As always, excessive currency movements one way tend to overshoot the other. Once the prevailing sentiment shifts, the market tends to look around for supporting evidence. One moment the size of the budget deficit and the consequent need for high real interest rates were used as reasons for buying dollars. The next moment the two deficits were 'out of control'.

The trade-weighted dollar reached its peak in early March 1985, at 45% above its 1980 average level. The effect of this was increased protectionist pressure within the US, which the administration wanted to resist. Trading partners worried that US policy was leading to unsustainable international imbalances and the rise of inflation. In New York in September 1985 the Group of Seven (a group of major Western industrialized nations) agreed to intervene to reduce the value of the dollar. This confirmed what the markets had already decided and in practice the task for central banks was to smooth the fall. By September 1986 the dollar had retraced about 30% of its rise. By February 1987, when the Louvre Accord was announced, it had fallen back to its 1980 level. The Accord was a sign that most central banks thought the fall had gone far enough and this probably had some temporary effect in slowing its further descent. After another sharp fall in March there was a period of reasonable strength in the summer before the announcement of the record June trade deficit in mid-August 1987. Only in 1988 are there signs that market sentiment may be shifting again. As the Republicans met to nominate Mr Bush, the dollar index was very close to its level when he took his oath as vice-president in 1981.

During this time the roller-coaster path of the dollar was reflected in the trade deficit which grew from about $40 billion in 1981 to $160 billion in 1987. Only in 1988 has there been a significant improvement. It would be wrong to put all the blame for this on the exchange rate. Some estimates have suggested that about a third of the trade deterioration could be put down to the effect of the deterioration in price competitiveness as a result of the dollar's rise. This has been reversed. But just as important is the difference in growth rates between the US and its major OECD trading partners. US domestic demand will need to grow more slowly if the trade balance is to continue to improve. Moreover, there are realistic limits to the impact on the trade account from improved export performance, particularly as the level of US imports is so much larger than exports. Although exchange rate changes are a powerful instrument for redressing external balances, and the fall in the dollar is reflected in trade volumes, there are also forces pressing in other directions. Most significantly, sustained, large current account deficits have turned the US into a net international debtor. By the end of the decade the country's net foreign debt could be some $500 billion.

At the start of the Reagan years the emphasis was upon supply-side economics: an economy stimulated by lower taxes and reduced government spending and by consequently increased personal savings. In the event, if there has been a supply-side 'miracle' it has been fostered by foreign money. The federal deficit has averaged just under 5% of GNP since 1982. Of this, the general government deficit has averaged 3–3.5% of GNP. Whilst this is well in line with other OECD countries, it is large compared both with America's private savings and its past experience. Hence the importance of attracting international savings.

The international nature of capital markets was brought home very dramatically by the collapse of world stock markets in October 1987. The fall started in the US where the immediate trigger was a set of disappointing trade figures. Panic swept the world markets when the comments and actions of leading figures in the US and West Germany were interpreted as casting doubt on the commitment to stabilize the dollar. It is impossible to say what causes sudden stock market movements of such scale but this latest brought into focus underlying concerns about the persistent US trade and budget deficits.

However, US economic performance since 1985 has been impressive and last October's stock market crash did very little to dent this. Growth in business investment has been significantly higher than the average for previous recoveries. Also, the relationship between growth and inflation has improved. Since the recovery began, real GNP has grown at an annual rate above 4%, which is significantly better than in most OECD countries. Rapid economic growth has been accompanied by rising living standards and increased productivity. The growth in employment has been faster than in previous expansions and the unemployment rate is now at its lowest level since 1974. Most important of all, amidst all this growth there is little evidence of accelerating inflation.

The legacy of the Reagan years is thus mixed, but the pluses probably outweigh the minuses. The economy is much stronger than it was when President Reagan came to office. But despite recent improvements, a cutback in domestic consumption is needed if the trade deficit is to become manageable. This does not mean that the US must go through another recession. Certain autonomous actions may ease the path; for example, consumers might decide to save more and rebuild their credit. This would reduce the reliance on foreign capital, but the continued need for growth in private investment will take its share of any additional savings. The most certain way to reduce domestic consumption is to reduce the budget deficit. Both candidates know this. Achieving it will be more a matter of political leadership than of economic analysis.

CHRONOLOGY OF PRINCIPAL EVENTS

DATE	FOREIGN	DOMESTIC

1981

DATE	FOREIGN	DOMESTIC
20 Jan	After 444 days of captivity, 52 American hostages in Iran are released within 24 hours of Reagan's inauguration, following an agreement to return $8 billion of frozen assets to the Ayatollah's regime.	
9 Feb	General Jaruzelski becomes Prime Minister of Poland.	
30 Mar		Assassination attempt on President Reagan by John W. Hinckley Jr, obsessive fan of actress Jodie Foster.
2 Apr	Heavy fighting breaks out in Lebanon between Arab forces and Lebanese right-wing militia.	
12 Apr		Successful launch of the first space shuttle, Columbia.
30 Apr	The National Party in South Africa is returned with a greatly reduced majority.	
5 May		Libyan diplomats expelled from the US.
13 May	Assassination attempt on the Pope by Turkish terrorist.	
14 Jun	USSR accuses Poland's trade union leaders of 'anti-Sovietism'.	
16 July	Israeli aircraft bomb Beirut.	
19 July		111 people killed when part of the Hyatt Hotel in Kansas collapses.
29 July		Congress passes Reagan's tax-cut legislation – the largest reduction in the nation's history.
3 Aug		Air traffic controllers begin illegal nationwide strike after rejecting government

offer of a new contract. Two days later most are dismissed after failing to return to work.

9 Aug Reagan announces plans to go ahead with the manufacture of the neutron bomb.

19 Aug US and Libya blame each other for air battle in the Gulf of Sirte. Two days later President Reagan declares the Gulf 'international waters'.

18 Sept USSR calls on Poland's leaders to crush anti-Soviet activities.

2 Oct The President announces plans for an increase in nuclear weapons.

Lech Walesa is elected Chairman of Solidarity. Ayatollah Khomenei is elected President of Iran.

6 Oct President Sadat of Egypt is assassinated.

21 Oct President Reagan blames Mr Brezhnev for distorting American policy, in particular, in remarks made about the possible use of tactical nuclear weapons.

4 Nov Secretary of State Alexander Haig says that NATO might fire a nuclear warning shot against USSR; Defense Secretary Casper Weinberger denies it.

30 Nov US and Israel sign a brief-lived agreement on 'strategic co-operation' – scrapped when Israel votes to annex the Golan Heights on 18 December.

1 Dec Soviet–US arms limitation talks begin in Geneva.

10 Dec President Reagan calls on

all US nationals to leave
Libya.

23 Dec   The President orders
sanctions against the new
Polish military government
in response to the
imposition of martial law on
14 December.

DATE	FOREIGN	DOMESTIC

1982

11 Jan   President Reagan assures
Mr Begin that the
differences between Israel
and the US are now 'a thing
of the past'.

4 Feb   US and USSR fail to reach
agreement on proposals for
arms reduction.

5 Feb   Major-General Chitov, the
senior officer at the Soviet
Embassy in Washington, is
expelled after being
accused of spying by the
FBI.

1 Mar   Ford car workers vote by
73% majority to give up pay
rises in favour of greater job
security over next 2 years.

2 Mar   Senate vote in favour of bill
to ban busing for the
purpose of racial
integration.

10 Mar   US totally bans Libyan oil
imports, accusing Libya of
continued terrorist policy
against Americans.

12 Apr   Deputy Secretary of State
Walter Stoessel goes to the
Middle East as fears of an
Israeli invasion of Lebanon
increase.

9 May   President Reagan proposes
a one-third reduction in
both Soviet and US ballistic
missiles.

10 June	Mrs Thatcher visits the White House for talks on the Falklands conflict.	
12 June		Mass demonstration in Central Park, New York, against nuclear arms.
25 June		Alexander Haig resigns as Secretary of State and is replaced by George Shultz.
20 July		Official figures show that over 31 million Americans are living below the poverty line and that spending power has declined by 3.5% in the last year.
23 July		Senate approves the largest tax increase in US history and cuts welfare spending.
22 Sept		President Reagan secures emergency powers from Congress to order striking train drivers back to work.
9 Oct	President Reagan ends Poland's favoured trade status in response to the decision formally to outlaw Solidarity.	
5 Nov		10.4% unemployment rate announced – the highest level since 1940.
10 Nov	Leonid Brezhnev dies of a heart attack at the age of 75. He is succeeded by Yuri Andropov.	
13 Nov	Lech Walesa, leader of Solidarity, released after 11 months' imprisonment. US resumes sales of oil and gas to USSR after 2 years' embargo, imposed in protest against the invasion of Afghanistan.	
16 Nov		Space shuttle Columbia completes its first operational flight.
7 Dec		House of Representatives votes to refuse funds for MX missile production.

DATE	FOREIGN	DOMESTIC
1983		
31 Jan		President Reagan offers to meet Mr Andropov to discuss a missile pact but the offer is rejected.
7 Feb	Iran launches a major offensive against Iraq.	
14 Mar	OPEC cuts crude oil prices.	
1 Apr	CND supporters in Britain link hands to form a chain between US bases at Burghfield and Greenham Common.	
6 Apr	France expels 47 Soviet diplomats for spying.	
8 Apr	USSR expels 2 British journalists.	
18 Apr	39 people killed in bomb blast at the US Embassy in Beirut.	
20 Apr		President Reagan signs compromise bill to prevent bankruptcy of the Social Security System.
1 May	Workers clash with police in Poland.	
17 May	Medium-range missile negotiations resume in Geneva.	
24 May		IRS granted right by Supreme Court to deny tax exemption to private schools which practise racial discrimination.
9 June	Margaret Thatcher re-elected as British Prime Minister.	
18 June		Challenger space shuttle launches with Sally Ride, the first American woman in space.
24 June	Yassir Arafat is ordered to leave Syria.	
6 July	Syria refuses to withdraw from Lebanon.	

22 July	Beirut airport shelled by Druze forces.
12 Aug	17 people killed in Chile in day of protest against President Pinochet.
27 Aug	Mr Andropov offers to destroy SS20s in return for US not deploying new missiles in Europe.
1 Sept	World-wide condemnation follows the USSR's shooting down of South Korean 747 jet over the Sea of Japan. All 269 passengers and crew are killed.
12 Sept	USSR expels US diplomat for spying.
3 Oct	Many PLO leaders desert the staff of Yassir Arafat.

4 Oct

President Reagan proposes a 'build down' nuclear arms deal.

10 Oct	Yitzhak Shamir takes office as Prime Minister of Israel.
23 Oct	300 members of the multinational peacekeeping force in Lebanon, including US marines and sailors, are killed by 2 members of the Free Islamic Revolutionary Movement driving a truck of explosives into their HQ at Beirut International Airport.
25 Oct	US troops invade the island of Grenada to depose the new Marxist regime but within a few days Congress decrees US Forces should leave the island by 24 December.

28 Oct

US oil rig sinks in South China Sea; all 61 on board are killed.

4 Nov	Bomb-laden truck is driven into the Israeli HQ in Lebanon, killing 60. Israel retaliates by bombing

Syrian and Druze positions.

14 Nov First Cruise missiles in Britain arrive at Greenham Common. 141 people arrested the next day for protesting outside the House of Commons.

11 Dec 30,000 women demonstrate around the perimeter fence of Greenham Common; 60 arrests are made.

27 Dec Record low temperatures kill 270 in America.

DATE	FOREIGN	DOMESTIC

1984

18 Jan President of the American University in Beirut is shot.

25 Jan President Reagan calls for budget cuts of $100 billion over next 3 years.

29 Jan President Reagan announces that he is seeking re-election, refuting doubts over his state of health.

7 Feb British troops leave Lebanon after US marines announce their withdrawal.

9 Feb Yuri Andropov dies in Moscow, aged 69. He is succeeded by Konstantin Chernenko, 3 years his senior, as President of the Soviet Union and General Secretary of the Communist Party.

26 Feb US marines withdraw from Beirut to offshore fleet.

14 Mar Record-breaking £500 million burst of trading on London Stock Exchange.

10 Apr CIA condemned by Congress and the Senate for taking part in the mining

		of Nicaraguan harbours.
22 Apr	Britain breaks diplomatic relations with Libya and expels Libyan diplomats following the shooting of WPC Fletcher outside the London Libyan People's Bureau.	
26 Apr	President Reagan visits China for the first time.	
2 May		President Reagan meets the Pope in Alaska.
8 May	Soviet Union withdraws from Los Angeles Olympic Games.	
1 June	President Reagan visits Ireland.	
8 June	World leaders meet in London for economic summit to endorse new approach to solution of the international debt crisis.	
1 July	USSR rejects President Reagan's offer to hold talks on banning weapons in space.	
12 July		Democratic presidential candidate Walter Mondale makes historic move in choosing a woman, Geraldine Ferraro, to run with him as candidate for vice-president.
23 Aug		President Reagan and Vice-President Bush renominated by the Republican convention.
24 Aug	Israeli election results in a hung parliament, with both parties trying to form a coalition.	
29 Aug		Opening ceremony of Los Angeles Olympic Games.
17 Sept		Dollar soars to new heights on the foreign exchange markets.
30 Sept	US and USSR agree to a 'process' for the regular	

	exchange of views to relieve international tension.	
31 Oct	Indira Gandhi is assassinated by 2 Sikh extremists in her bodyguard.	
6 Nov		President Reagan re-elected for second term of office.
9 Nov	Nicaragua calls for an emergency session of the UN Security Council after claiming an American invasion threat.	
6 Dec	Hijackers of a Kuwaiti airliner kill 4 hostages in Tehran. Two days later Iranian security forces release the other 9 hostages.	

DATE	FOREIGN	DOMESTIC
1985		
16 Feb	Israeli troops withdraw from Sidon area of Lebanon.	
10 Mar	Konstantin Chernenko dies, aged 73. He is succeeded by Mikhail Gorbachev, at 54, the youngest member of the Politburo.	
14 Mar	5-year-old Iraq–Iran war enters new phase as both sides bomb civilian areas across the borders.	
28 Mar		House of Representatives gives final authorization for deployment of controversial MX missiles.
22 Apr	British diplomats expelled from Moscow, as are their counterparts in London.	
26 Apr	US expels Soviet military attaché.	
11 June	23 people previously jailed	

	in the Eastern bloc exchanged in Berlin for 4 Eastern Europeans arrested for spying in the US.	
15 June	Shi'ite Moslem extremists hijack TWA flight from Athens to Rome. Two Americans badly beaten, 1 shot and 39 hostages held in Beirut until 30 June.	
10 July	1,745 people die after inhaling poisonous fumes from the Union Carbide factory in Bhopal.	
11 July	Senate votes to impose economic sanctions on South Africa in protest against apartheid. After increasing violence in black townships, South African government declares a state of emergency.	
13 July		President Reagan undergoes surgery for cancer, making a rapid recovery.
	Live Aid concert in Philadelphia and London raises record amount of money for drought-stricken peoples of Africa.	
11 Aug		135 people injured when toxic gas escapes from Union Carbide plant in US.
19 Sept	20–30,000 killed in Mexican earthquake.	
7 Oct	*Achille Lauro* cruise ship hijacked just off Port Said by 5 members of the Palestine Liberation Front. 69-year-old disabled American man is shot dead and thrown overboard. Three days later Egypt reports that the hijackers have surrendered into the hands of the PLO but American fighter jets force	

14 Nov	their plane to land in Sicily. 23,000 killed in volcanic eruption in Columbia.	
19 Nov	President Reagan and Mr Gorbachev hold summit conference in Geneva. Gorbachev declares: 'The world has become a safer place.'	
23 Nov	Egyptian jet hijacked by Arab terrorists between Athens and Cairo. 60 of the 98 passengers and crew are killed before the hijackers are overcome.	
12 Dec		Gramm–Rudman–Hollings Act signed by President Reagan in desperate attempt to bring federal deficit under control.
27 Dec	Palestinian terrorists kill 20 civilians in attacks on El Al and TWA desks at airports in Rome and Vienna.	

DATE	FOREIGN	DOMESTIC
1986		
1 Jan	President Reagan and Mr Gorbachev swap TV pledges of peace.	
3 Jan	US task force sails for Libya.	
8 Jan	All Libyan assets frozen in US.	
20 Jan		New holiday, Martin Luther King Day, celebrated for first time.
28 Jan		Space shuttle Challenger explodes shortly after take-off, killing 6 astronauts and a New Hampshire teacher.
7 Feb	Jean-Claude Duvalier flees to France, ending his family's 29-year dictatorship of Haiti.	
11 Feb	Soviet dissident Anatoly	

	Scharansky is freed in Berlin.	
25 Feb	President Ferdinand Marcos of the Philippines is airlifted to Hawaii by US. Corazon Aquino succeeds him, claiming genuine election victory.	
14 Apr	US fighter jets from British bases bomb Libyan targets in Tripoli and Benghazi.	
28 Apr	Major disaster at Chernobyl nuclear power plant in USSR is not reported by Soviet officials for 3 days.	
12 June		US officials predict tenfold rise in AIDS cases within 5 years.
4 July		President Reagan unveils Statue of Liberty after refurbishments costing $171 million.
7 July		Gramm–Rudman–Hollings Act provision for 'balanced budget' declared unconstitutional by Supreme Court.
15 July	President Reagan agrees to SALT 2 talks in Geneva.	
31 Aug	US journalist, Nicholas Daniloff, arrested by Soviets for spying.	
5 Sept	US aircraft is hijacked in Karachi; 18 of the 400 passengers are killed as Pakistani commandos storm the plane.	
29 Sept	Nicholas Daniloff and 2 dissidents freed after Gennady Zakharov is accused of spying and expelled from New York.	
10 Oct	890 killed in earthquake in El Salvador.	
11 Oct	President Reagan and Mr Gorbachev hold arms talks in Iceland. 'Star Wars' issue blocks progress. Expulsion	

	of diplomats on both sides follows.	
22 Oct		Tax Reform Act signed by the President.
25 Nov		Vice-Admiral John Poindexter resigns and Lt-Col Oliver North is sacked over the Iran–Contra affair.
8 Dec		Iran–Contra hearings begin in Washington.
11 Dec	South Africa imposes sweeping restrictions on press, radio and television reporting.	
14 Dec		America fails to reach America's Cup final for first time in 135 years.

DATE	FOREIGN	DOMESTIC
1987		
21 Jan	Terry Waite disappears in Beirut.	
10 Feb	Kremlin releases 140 dissidents. Five days later Josif Begun is released from prison.	
26 Feb		Tower Report concludes President Reagan failed to control Iran arms deals but did not deliberately lie.
4 Mar		President Reagan accepts full responsibility for direction of funds to the Contras.
14 Apr	President Reagan invites Mr Gorbachev to Washington for a third summit.	
8 May		Gary Hart withdraws from race for US presidency in shadow of sex scandal with model, Donna Rice, only 3 days after announcing his intention to run for office.
17 May	37 American sailors are killed when the USS *Stark*	

is hit by an Exocet missile in the Gulf.

29 May West German student, Mathias Rust, lands a light aircraft in Red Square, causing embarrassment to Soviet security forces.

11 June British Prime Minister, Margaret Thatcher, is returned to office for a third term.

21 June Local government elections held in USSR for the first time in decades.

8 July Oliver North gives evidence at the Iran–Contra hearings, saying that the scheme seemed 'a neat idea' and he 'assumed' it had been approved by the President through his superiors but he had never personally discussed it with Reagan.

20 July UN Security Council pass Resolution 598 calling for a ceasefire in the Gulf.

21 July US flag hoisted on 2 Kuwaiti tankers in the Gulf. Three days later the US tanker *Bridgeton* is struck by an Iranian mine.

31 July Over 400 Iranian pilgrims are killed in Mecca. Iranian officials allege a US/Saudi conspiracy.

11 Aug British and French decide to send task forces to the Gulf for protection of civilian shipping.

18 Aug US hostage Charles Glass reappears in Beirut, claiming to have escaped whilst his captors slept.

17 Sept Josif Begun and family are told they can leave USSR for Israel.

Bicentenary celebrations of the US Constitution.

DATE	FOREIGN	DOMESTIC
17 Oct		Infant Jessica McClure is rescued after spending 58 hours down a well in Texas.
19 Oct	World financial markets, including Wall Street, take a dive on 'Black Monday'.	
5 Nov		Casper Weinberger resigns as Defense Secretary.
	Mrs Thatcher asks President Reagan to reduce US budget deficit.	
18 Nov		Congress blames President Reagan over Iran–Contra affair, accusing him of failing in his constitutional duty to uphold the law.
8 Dec	Reagan and Gorbachev sign INF Treaty at Washington summit.	
15 Dec		Gary Hart re-enters presidential election campaign.
18 Dec		Ivan Boesky jailed for 3 years for insider trading on New York Stock Exchange.

DATE	FOREIGN	DOMESTIC
1988		
1 Jan	New Year speeches by President Reagan and Mr Gorbachev are carried by TV in both countries.	
25 Jan		George Bush clashes with anchorman, Dan Rather, in live TV news interview.
26 Jan		In his State of the Union address, President Reagan urges Congress to continue aid to the Contras; to ratify INF Treaty signed at Washington summit; and to support SDI programme.
29 Jan		The President signs order to end concessions on imports from Hong Kong, South Korea, Singapore and

		Thailand.
4 Feb		Federal grand juries in Miami and Tampa indict General Noriega of Panama on charges of violating US racketeering and drug laws.
8 Feb		Iowa caucuses: George Bush forced into third place behind Dole and Robertson. Dukakis finishes third behind Gephardt and Simon.
9 Feb	In London, US and UK sign agreement on confiscation of assets from drug traffickers.	
11 Feb	Ethnic unrest becomes violent in Soviet regions of Armenia and Azerbaijan.	
16 Feb		New Hampshire primary: Bush rebounds to beat Dole. Dukakis is also a big winner for the Democrats.
18 Feb		Babbitt and du Pont quit the presidential race.
3 Mar		Panamanian assets in US frozen in an attempt to pressurize General Noriega into resignation.
	NATO extraordinary summit agrees to keep US nuclear weapons 'up to date' in Europe 'where necessary'.	
		House of Representatives rejects proposal to provide aid to the Contras for the first time since 1984.
8 Mar		Super Tuesday: Bush sweeps Republican votes in the primaries. For the Democrats, the result is a stalemate.
11 Mar		Gary Hart withdraws from the presidential election race again.
22 Mar		Congress over-rules President's veto of Grove City civil rights bill.

23 Mar	Nicaraguan peace talks begin between Defence Minister General Humberto Ortega Saavedra and Contra leader Adolfo Robelo.	
26 Mar		Jackson wins a landslide victory in Michigan caucuses.
28–9 Mar		Gephardt and Dole withdraw from the race.
5 Apr	Kuwaiti aircraft hijacked over Iran and taken to Cyprus and then Algeria. Two hostages killed during 15-day seige before Algerians negotiate the release of the remaining hostages in exchange for hijackers' freedom.	
		Dukakis scores a breakthrough victory in Wisconsin primary, beating Jackson by 48% to 28%.
13 Apr	Group of Seven industrialized nations reaffirm their commitment to the Feb 1987 Louvre Accord on Currency Stability in an attempt to prevent the dollar falling further on foreign exchange markets.	
18 Apr	US naval patrol in Gulf attacks Iranian vessels and oil platforms in response to Iranian mine-damage and attacks on US ships.	
2 May		Donald Regan's memoirs allege that Nancy Reagan and her astrological convictions dominate the President's actions.
11 May		President Reagan endorses George Bush; Robertson announces he will suspend his campaign.
29 May–		

2 June	Ratification documents on INF Treaty signed and Strategic Weapon Reduction Treaty drafted at Moscow summit.	
7 June		Dukakis concludes primary season by clinching sufficient delegates to carry the Democratic nomination.
3 July	USS *Vincennes* shoots down Iranian airbus in the Gulf, killing 290 passengers and crew. President Reagan expresses his 'deep regret' at the incident.	
5 July		Attorney-General Edwin Meese resigns after mounting allegations of unethical conduct.
11 July	The President announces that ex-gratia payments will be made to the families bereaved in the airbus incident, administered through a neutral third party to ensure that none of the settlements fall into the hands of the Iranian Government.	
18-21 July		Democratic convention in Atlanta nominates Michael Dukakis for presidential candidate and Lloyd Bentsen as vice-presidential candidate. Jackson's initial bitterness at being passed over is salved.
3 Aug		President Reagan calls Michael Dukakis an 'invalid' following allegations that the latter has received treatment for mental disorders in the past. He quickly retracts the remark and claims it was a joke that didn't work. Dukakis's family doctor

	denies allegations of any psychiatric treatment and gives a summary of his patient's medical history over the past 17 years.
5 Aug	Bush's campaign for the presidency gets a boost from two fronts: Possible controversy is shelved when Colonel Oliver North's trial for the Iran–Contra affair is delayed until after the presidential election. There are disputes over secret documents North has demanded be produced in evidence. Treasury Secretary James Baker announces that he will resign on 17 Aug to become chairman of George Bush's campaign.
15–18 Aug	Republican convention in New Orleans bids President Reagan farewell. He endorses Bush, saying 'George played a major role in everything we've accomplished.' Bush picks Senator Dan Quayle as his vice-presidential running mate, amidst controversy over Quayle's military service in the National Guard.
17 Aug	General Zia ul-Haq, President of Pakistan, is killed when his plane explodes shortly after take-off. Two of his closest military advisers and the US Ambassador to Pakistan are also among the dead.

CHAPTER TWO

The Political Background

THE SEPARATION OF POWERS

This November Americans will elect not only a president, but also a third of the Senate and all of the House of Representatives. The president has no power to dissolve Congress and the Congress, short of impeachment, cannot remove the president from office. Politically they depend on each other to be able to work effectively but under the Constitution they have separate powers and distinct functions. The term 'separation of powers' is familiar to a British audience, with our traditional division of authority between the Crown, Judiciary and Parliament, but the differences between these various elements in Britain and those in the United States are real and important.

The former Lord Chancellor, Lord Hailsham, once spoke of the threat to our system of 'elective dictatorship'. By this he meant that Britain has a political system in which party discipline ensures that the will of the majority party in the Commons normally prevails regardless of public opinion. Thus, in Britain, the Cabinet (in effect the Executive) and Parliament (the Legislature), are, whatever constitutional theory may say, effectively one. Whilst the Crown has the ultimate sanction of refusing to assent to a parliamentary bill, this power is unlikely to be used except *in extremis*. The power afforded to the British prime minister, bolstered by a majority in the House of Commons, is therefore much greater than the US Constitution allows its president.

As this section explains, power in America is, as the Founding Fathers intended, split between Congress and the president and between Washington and the states. Sometimes the different parts of government work together, sometimes against each other. But when the system operates as it was intended each part provides a check and balance on the others. In practical political terms the continuing success of the US system rests in large measure upon the *real* separation of the executive and legislature; the different size of the electoral bases of those returned to the House, Senate and presidency; the various timings of their elections (one-third of senators elected every two years; the entire House elected every two years; the president elected every four years – with the 22nd Amendment preventing more than two terms) making it difficult for anyone to claim a 'mandate'; and the weakness of the party system which limits the President to exercising 'influence' rather than 'control' over Congress.

A President of the United States has no guaranteed majority in the legislature and cannot fundamentally alter the powers of the states. Also, many of the powers of the modern presidency flow from specific congressional authorizations, the terms of which provide for subsequent congressional oversight of the executive. To succeed, whoever is elected to the White House this November will have to work with and sometimes compromise with the other parts of government.

President Kennedy summed up the differences between our two systems: 'The President ... is rightly described as a man of extraordinary powers. Yet it is also true that he must wield those powers under extraordinary limitations.' The experience of the present incumbent of the Oval Office is most instructive. Ronald Reagan has undoubtedly been one of the most popular presidents in many years. His personal authority was stamped upon the US invasion of Grenada; the air-strike against Libya; the promotion of SDI as a defence system; and the budget and tax cuts which went through Congress in 1981. Yet, in his term we have also seen, through the power of television, relatively junior congressmen seize the political platform in a way which would have startled his predecessors. In addition, as government has become more complex we have seen the growth, both in numbers and power, of presidential aides. At its most extreme we saw, in the Iran–Contra scandal, National Security Advisor John Poindexter bypass cabinet secretaries and usurp the power of the President himself.

As Republican Representative Newt Gingrich of Georgia put it:

> What you have right now is a constitutional monarchy. What we've done is we've reinvented Hanoverian kingship without reinventing the parliamentary prime ministership. We have this tremendously nice, likeable King Victoria. Everybody likes him but where the hell's Disraeli or Gladstone?

The President
The President of the United States is elected once every four years and is only allowed to serve two terms. The Constitution has surprisingly little to say about his powers. Set out in Article 2, they

are neither very numerous nor clearly stated. But if the constitutional language was left vague, holders of the presidency over the last two hundred years have filled in the gaps and extended presidential actions and powers well beyond what the Founding Fathers would have expected.

The Constitution gives the president the 'executive power'. It makes him commander-in-chief of the armed forces and grants him the power to make treaties with the advice of the Senate. It also says that 'from time to time' he will give Congress information on the State of the Union and that he shall see that the 'laws are faithfully executed'.

To help the president, government departments were soon established. There are now thirteen departments – Agriculture, Commerce, Defense, Education, Energy, Health and Human Services, Housing and Urban Development, Interior, Justice, Labor, State (the equivalent of our Foreign Office), Transportation, and Treasury. The secretaries who make up the Cabinet are directly answerable to the president and do not normally have their own independent political bases. They cannot be members of Congress. They serve only for as long as the president continues to have confidence in them. However, it is also important to remember that the entire executive branch is created and funded by Congress and thus presidential power over them is balanced by 'departmental' congressional committees.

Nowadays in addition to the departments headed by the secretaries there are many semi-autonomous federal agencies employing millions of people whom the president has the responsibility of co-ordinating (e.g. the Environmental Protection Agency, Federal Reserve Board, Veterans Administration, etc.).

One of the most important agencies is the Office of Management and Budget. It prepares the budget which the president presents to Congress. Although Congress does not necessarily accept the executive branch's figures, it has given the presidency powers this century which enable it to play a major role in the budget process.

The president appoints Supreme Court justices, subject to the approval of the Senate. Presidents tend to appoint people whom they think will be politically sympathetic. There is, therefore, a tendency for the court to reflect changing political trends. This should not, however, be exaggerated. There are nine justices, each of whom can serve for life. The turnover rate is low and so a president normally has to be in office for some considerable time before he can have a major impact on the court's composition. Senate approval is not a mere formality either, as President Reagan knows. He wanted to appoint the conservative jurist Robert Bork to the court, but the Senate Judiciary Committee blocked him. Judge Ginsberg was the next presidential nominee but his name was withdrawn in advance of certain rejection. The President finally had to settle for the much more moderate Justice Kennedy.

Justices themselves have also historically shown considerable independence from the presidents who appointed them. The best example of that was Chief Justice Earl Warren. A former Republican Governor of California and Thomas Dewey's running mate in the 1948 presidential election, President Eisenhower thought he would act as a conservative in the court. He turned out to be the most liberal chief justice of the court's history. Eisenhower described the appointment as the biggest mistake he ever made.

The presidency nowadays plays a major part in the legislative process. The Constitution clearly gives the legislative power to Congress and in the nineteenth century presidents saw their role as executing laws that Congress initiated and passed. But in recent years this century the White House has been regularly expected to have its own programme for which the president tries to persuade, cajole and bully congressional support (Eisenhower, in 1953, was the last president to decline to present such a programme). Landmark legislation such as Roosevelt's New Deal laws or the Kennedy–Johnson civil rights programme would not have reached the statute books without presidential action.

One of the important powers the president has in getting his way on legislation is the actual or more often the threatened use of his veto. The president can veto a whole bill, though not individual parts of it, and his veto can only be overturned by obtaining a two-thirds majority in both houses of Congress.

The Founding Fathers intended Congress to play a considerable role in conducting the United States' foreign policy. Congress was given the authority to declare war and the Senate the power to ratify treaties as well as approve ambassadorial appointments. But during the nineteenth century the presidency came to play the major role in foreign policy and in 1936 this was to a great extent formalized when the Supreme Court ruled that the executive branch, and the executive branch alone, has the right to negotiate with foreign countries.

Allied to the president's leading role in conducting foreign policy is his position as commander-in-chief of the armed forces. Successive American presidents have sent troops into combat without seeking prior congressional authority. The Korean and Vietnam wars were both examples of the president acting without a formal declaration of war. The president does of course need congressional support for appropriations for the armed forces, but, as Vietnam showed, once the executive has committed American military might it is very difficult for Congress not to continue to fund it. The congressional passage of the Gulf of Tonkin resolution in

1964 provided the legal basis for subsequent US action in Vietnam; there were no dissenting votes in the House and just two in the Senate.

The Congress

Congress is divided into two separate houses with equal legislative powers. The Senate has 100 members, two from each state regardless of size or population. Each senator is elected for a six-year term with one-third of the Senate coming up for election every two years. The senator first elected for a particular state is known as the Senior Senator, and his colleague as the Junior Senator. The House of Representatives has 435 members, known as Congressmen or Representatives. Their districts are roughly equal in population. The entire House is elected every two years.

The bicameral structure of Congress reflects the equality of states irrespective of size or population in the Senate, and the varying population of states in the House. For example, whilst California and Wyoming each have two senators, the former has 45 representatives, and the latter, only one. It is therefore not necessarily the case that the Senate reflects local interests in the way that the House always does: populous states such as California, New York and Texas vary greatly within their own borders and these variations are reflected in the different interests and opinions of the large number of representatives they return to the House.

Article 1 of the Constitution lists the powers vested in Congress. Its main responsibility is to legislate. A bill can be introduced in either chamber and must have been passed by both in an identical form before it can become law. If the bill emerges from the two chambers amended in different ways, then a conference is set up between the relevant committees of the House and the Senate to hammer out a compromise. A lot of legislation is nowadays initiated by the administration but it must pass through Congress before it can become law. When legislation has been agreed in Congress the bill is presented to the president. At this stage he has three options:

1. To sign the bill, in which case it becomes law;
2. To do nothing. If after ten days during which Congress is in session the president has not returned a bill with his objections, the Constitution states that it becomes law as though he had signed it. Presidents sometimes do nothing because they object to a bill but do not have enough support to veto it;
3. To veto it. Congress can over-ride the veto, but a two-thirds majority is required in both chambers.

In addition, the Constitution gives the Senate a number of powers to check presidential action. Top federal appointments are made by the president but only on 'the advice and consent' of the Senate. The Senate therefore can, and on occasion does, reject presidential choices. Appointments to federal posts within a state where a senator is from the same party as the president are made only after consultation with the senator.

In the field of foreign affairs Congress normally gives the president a fairly free hand. But the Senate can if it chooses check his actions. All treaties must get two-thirds approval from the Senate before they can commit the United States to a course of action. President Carter failed to obtain approval on SALT 2. President Reagan took great care to carry key senators with him when he negotiated the INF treaty. To an extent presidents have got around the problem of the two-thirds requirement by making agreements with foreign powers by 'executive order', but most prefer the added authority of a treaty.

The States

Powers are not only separated within the federal government in Washington but are also divided between Washington and the states. Unlike Britain, where local government derives its powers from Parliament and has no independent standing in terms of constitutional law, there are powers that are specifically denied to both the president and Congress and are reserved for the separate states.

The American states have authority over a whole range of matters that in a unitary state such as the United Kingdom are the responsibility of central government. In America for instance, it is up to each individual state to decide whether or not to have the death penalty.

The states also greatly influence the composition and direction of the federal government itself. The Senate is, as described above, made up of two senators from each state, regardless of size. This makes the chamber a powerful voice for the states. It is conscious of the particular interests of states and plays a significant role in the preservation of their independence.

Similarly the members of the House of Representatives are very aware of local demands. It is not normal practice, as in Britain, for a politician to go in search of a constituency that will have him. Rather he must take his chances where he lives. This means that congressmen must respond to parochial interests, especially as they all face re-election every two years.

THE PARTIES

It is important to remember that the American political parties do not have direct counterparts in Britain, or indeed anywhere else in the world. They are formed on the basis of historical and regional conditions peculiar to the United States. It should be noted too that 'Democrat' and 'Republican' can stand for very different things in different states of this vast country. However, especially at the time of a presidential election – which is the only major nationwide political contest – it is possible to say something about what supporters and candidates of any particular party are *likely* to stand for.

Republicans are likely to be more conservative and right wing than Democrats. They have a not-entirely-deserved image of wealth and high incomes. They are more likely to favour business than labour unions, to support policies which reduce the sphere of the state, welfare payments, and the taxation that pays for it. They are likely to have the reputation for encouraging low federal government spending.

They are likely to be 'moral' conservatives, supporting traditional family values. Fundamentalist Christians form one of the strongest Republican groups in presidential elections. It is worth remembering that the opposite of 'conservative' in the US is 'liberal'.

In foreign affairs, Republicans tend to be more vigorously anti-Communist, in favour of aiding the Contras in Nicaragua, for example. Their commitment to military expenditure cuts against their traditional dislike of government spending. Once Republicans tended to be 'isolationist', but now they realize that the world is too small for that: an active military presence is required.

Traditionally, the Republican leadership was made up of 'WASPs' – White Anglo-Saxon Protestants. It is still true that many 'ethnic' groups do not feel the Republicans to be their natural party, but political conservatism, especially among Cubans and some Italian-Americans, cuts across that.

The Republicans can be expected to do well in the western and Rocky Mountain states, the Great Plains of the Midwest, in southern California and upstate New York, and, in a presidential election, the Deep South.

Democrats are traditionally more 'liberal' than Republicans, favouring higher government expenditure, more federal intervention, and greater support for labour unions and employees vis-à-vis employers.

In foreign affairs, Democrats are less likely to spend money on anti-Communist intervention or new defence programmes, though it should be noted that the First and Second World Wars, as well as the wars in Korea and Vietnam, were all entered by Democratic presidents.

Democrats obtain the vast majority of the black vote, and most of that of other 'ethnic groups' such as Hispanics (especially Puerto Ricans), Jews, and Irish and Italian Catholics. Lower-income groups and the less well educated are predominantly Democrat. They are particularly numerous in the inner cities, and in 'ethnic' parts of New England, northern California and Hawaii. It should be noted that in local elections the white Deep South still largely follows its tradition of voting Democrat, which goes back to the Civil War, but that this has not been translated into presidential support very frequently in the last two decades.

Although Democrats (outside the South) are more likely to be on the 'left' of the American political spectrum than Republicans, it should be stressed that they are in no way a socialist party. They fully support the capitalist enterprise culture of the USA.

ETHNIC VOTERS

In the continental United States where, except for small, scattered pockets of indigenous Indians and Inuits, everyone is either an immigrant or descended from immigrants, virtually the entire population can be divided into ethnic groups. And immigration continues apace, although the pattern is forever changing. The 1980 census showed that, among foreign-born US citizens, 65% of those who came from Europe arrived before 1960, whereas 69% of those from Asia and 58% of those from Central America have settled since 1970. This section concentrates mainly upon the two largest ethnic groups: blacks and Hispanics.

Black voters

According to the US Bureau of the Census, there were 29,306,000 blacks in the United States in 1986, representing 12.2% of the population. However, the Bureau has been accused of under-estimating the number of both blacks and Hispanics in the population, especially in the major cities. What is not disputed is that, in proportion to their share of the overall population, far fewer blacks vote than whites.

Black registration increased following the great voter-registration drives of the civil rights campaigns in the 1960s, only to decline in the early 1970s. Further drives since the mid-1970s have contributed both to greater black registration and higher turnout. However, starting from a low base, black turnout has lagged significantly behind white turnout (in 1980 it was 51% compared with 61% for whites). The economic recession of 1982 resulted in an increased turnout in the mid-term elections that year (the first increase in such elections in twenty years). A large element of that increased vote came from the black community and helped gain the Democrats 26 House seats as welll as a number of governorships. Yet, following the 1982 elections, the Bureau of the Census estimated that more than 7 million blacks were still not registered to vote.

That same year Kevin Phillips wrote in his book, *Post-Conservative America* (Random House, New York):

> Blacks constitute 11% of the national population, but cast only 7% of the total ballots in 1980.... One can reasonably suggest that the economic bottom third of the country cast only 20–25% of the total vote, while the top third cast perhaps 40–45%. This is a much greater imbalance than exists in any other major Western industrial nation.... To protect transfer payments and government spending programs, low-income and minority turnout has the potential to surge. These voters could also come to the polls to protest conservative economic policies tailored to redistribute income towards upper rather than lower income groups. Of all the trends that will affect the 1980s, this could be the most important.

About half of the country's voting-age blacks live in the South. Only about 16% of the southern voting-age population is black but their votes are disproportionately significant because they vote so overwhelmingly Democrat. (National exit poll evidence from the 1980 and 1984 presidential elections suggest that they voted 85% and 90% respectively for the Democrats.) To offset that advantage the Republicans need to secure a high percentage of the white vote. In recent presidential elections they have done so very successfully but, in a close race, the South begins to look more vulnerable for them (ABC News exit poll data from the 1984 election showed Mondale receiving 90% of the black vote in the South and Reagan 10%, whereas Reagan took 71% of the southern white vote, compared with 29% for Mondale). In the 1986 mid-term election the Democrats won five Senate seats in the South, following a concerted registration drive among blacks. Turnout was significantly lower then than it will be this November but a number of polls over this summer showed Dukakis much closer to Bush than Mondale was to Reagan in the South last time.

A key change this year has been the polarization of the black vote in the primaries. In a poll published in October 1983, Walter Mondale received the support of 36% of black voters compared with 46% for Jesse Jackson. However, looking at the evidence of CBS News exit polls for the Super Tuesday primaries in the South, Jesse Jackson won 90% or more of the black vote in all of them except Texas, where he won 89% and Maryland, where he won 88%.

Jackson posed a problem for the Democrats throughout his 1988 primary campaign: on the one hand polling evidence showed that he would be a serious liability as either the presidential or vice-presidential candidate (a poll for the US News and World Report sampled at the end of March found that 64% of people interviewed thought the country was not ready to elect Jesse Jackson as president); but on the other hand, the black voters he leads will be an important component of any Democratic victory in November. His speech at the Democratic convention, where he said, 'Shall we expand, be inclusive, find unity and power, or suffer division and impotence? Common ground, that is the challenge of our party tonight', occasioned great relief among party leaders. For black voters are not only important in the South. In each of three of the largest states in the Union – California, New York and Illinois – there are more than a million black voters and they comprise 25% or more of the population of such cities as Baltimore, Chicago, Cleveland, Detroit, Kansas City, Newark, Philadelphia and St Loius.

It is certain that black voters will vote overwhelmingly Democrat this November. The only problem the party faces is in mobilizing them in even greater numbers than in the past. The difficulty is that they are such a bedrock of Democratic voting that they do not feature in strategic calculations about the swings needed for the party to win the White House. The Democrats clearly need them but their previous solid support did not stop the Republicans winning four out of the last five presidential elections. The challenge for Michael Dukakis this year is to retain the black vote whilst regaining a substantial slice of the majority of the white vote which the Democrats lost in 1968, 1972, 1980 and 1984.

Hispanic voters

The Hispanic population amounted to 18,091,000 in 1986 (about 8% of the US population), according to the US Bureau of the Census (again, a figure which has been criticized as understating the real number). This total has doubled since 1970. Bureau projections suggest that by the year 2000 the number will rise to more than 25 million. In 1986, 81.5% of Hispanics were aged 44 years or less.

Whilst blacks in the US have a cohesive racial consciousness, the Hispanic community is much more diverse, often reflecting the individual's place of origin (or that of their parents) – there are Cubans, Mexican-Americans, Puerto Ricans and others from a variety of Spanish-speaking countries. They are more politically fragmented and volatile than the black population. Whilst they are more Democratic than Republican, their support for the party in recent years is nothing like as monolithic as that of the black population. There are also 'national' differences: Cuban-

Americans are more likely to vote Republican and Mexican-Americans are more likely to vote Democrat.

According to CBS News exit polls, 82% of Hispanics voted Democrat in 1976; but, in 1980, this figure fell significantly to 59%. The ABC News exit poll in 1984 revealed that 56% of Hispanics had voted Democrat. However, their electoral volatility is shown in the NBC News exit poll for the 1982 congressional elections when only 16% voted Republican.

Whilst Hispanics present a growing pool of voters which both parties are interested in attracting, they have shown an even greater reluctance to vote than blacks. Surveys conducted by the Bureau of the Census following the last two presidential elections revealed that, among Hispanics, only 36% claimed to be registered in 1980 and 40% in 1984 (compared with 67% and 68% respectively of all citizens). And when the Bureau asked who had actually voted in both elections, 30% of Hispanics claimed to have done so in 1980 and 33% in 1984.

Although Hispanics may be diverse politically, they are concentrated geographically. In *Post-Conservative America*, Kevin Phillips commented:

> The Sun Belt states of Florida, Texas and California, emerging as the linchpin of conservative politics in the 1980s, rank among the major US focal points of Third World (principally Hispanic) immigration. As of the early 1980s, Hispanics cast only a small percentage of the vote in all three states, well below their portion of the population. But if immigration continues, if relative fertility rates hold, and if Hispanic political awareness mushrooms, making the 1980s the 'Decade of the Hispanic' as predicted, the political equation in these pivotal states could change – greatly.

According to the 1980 census, Hispanics comprised 21% of the population of Texas, 19% in California and 9% in Florida (and they also comprised 37% of the population of the small state of New Mexico). Given their age profile and high birth-rate these percentages must have increased since then.

Clearly, Michael Dukakis will be using his fluent Spanish a great deal before November.

THE ISSUES

This section sets out some of the major issues facing America today and reviews what public opinion has to say about them. Clearly, the ratings and views expressed in the opinion poll data used not only pre-date the traditional starting point of the presidential election campaign (Labor Day, 5 September) but may also change during the campaign itself. Therefore, it is important to note that what follows offers no more and no less than a series of snapshots of American public opinion over the past twelve months.

Perhaps the most significant finding for both candidates was the response to the Harris poll in April 1988 which asked: 'Whoever is elected President in 1988 will have to decide whether to break with the past or whether to continue in the direction we are headed. Would you like to see the next President start with new policies or keep us headed in the same direction?' 66% of those polled opted for breaking with the past and starting with new policies.

The Economy: The public's perception of the US economy in general and its effects upon them individually are mixed. As Robert Waller states in Chapter One, their concerns have also changed considerably since the first Reagan presidency. In 1982 Gallup found 49% of Americans concerned that inflation and high prices were the most important problems facing the country: 28% nominated unemployment and the recession. By May this year those figures had fallen dramatically to 8% and 2% respectively. Even concern about the budget deficit, regarded by 14% as the most important problem in 1985, had almost halved to 8% by this May.

A real divergence exists between public perception of the prospects for the national economy and perception of personal prospects. Historically, the American public tends to be pessimistic about the economy even when it is doing well. In December 1987 a Harris poll asked respondents whether they thought that 'the economy will slump, with unemployment rising and prices also rising', and found 55% agreeing and 40% disagreeing. A July ABC News poll showed that only 23% of respondents thought the economy was getting better, whilst 36% thought it was getting worse. These two figures are important because ABC found that 73% of the former planned to vote for Bush and 68% of the latter intended to vote for Dukakis. Those who thought the economy was staying about the same divided almost evenly between the two candidates.

Yet, when ABC asked respondents in May about the state of their personal finances, 56% described them as either excellent or good, compared with 30% who opted for not so good or poor.

When it comes to the question of which party would do a better job of keeping the country prosperous, Gallup polls have registered a strong Republican lead throughout the period 1984-6. But this lead narrowed in 1987, and by May this year, 41% of those questioned nominated the Republicans and 39% the Democrats. As for the candidates themselves, a July NBC News poll among registered voters found an effective dead heat between the two regarding which was thought better able to handle the nation's economic problems.

Trade: Resentment against unfair trade practices by foreign governments and companies has grown along with the trade deficit (a record $160 billion last year) and the consequent closure of factories and loss of jobs. In late January NBC found 46% of Americans favouring a tax on imported oil, compared with 40% who were opposed. An NBC poll at the very beginning of March found that 55% of respondents thought a limit on imported goods would help the country (29% thought it would hurt America). And 54% of those same respondents favoured greater limits on imported goods even if it increased prices (34% opposed). Democratic candidate Richard Gephardt made the issue of unfair foreign trade practices the most high-profile issue of his campaign. His candidature failed but public feeling on the subject did not sink with him.

CBS News exit polls in the Super Tuesday states asked voters whether economic competition from other countries had helped, hurt, or had little impact on their community. In each state significantly more thought their community had been hurt rather than helped and this assessment was shared by Democratic and Republican voters. In June, NBC found 81% of respondents agreeing that there should be a law requiring the President to take tougher action on this issue. When they were reminded that President Reagan had vetoed such a law, 69% disagreed with his action. In the public's view, the perceived encroachment of foreign companies into the American economy is allied to unfair foreign trade policy. A July NBC poll found 84% of registered voters agreeing that foreign countries have too much control over America's economy.

Taxation: One of the central charges which will be levelled against the Democrats in this year's campaign is that they are the party of higher taxation. In 1984 Walter Mondale actually volunteered the information that he would raise the level of federal taxes. In 1988 Michael Dukakis has refused to rule out the possibility of some increase in taxes in the future whilst George Bush has pledged not to raise them. Clearly, taxation is a sensitive problem for any politician but the American public seems to view their promises on this subject with a degree of scepticism. When ABC dealt with taxation in their July poll they informed respondents of the candidates' positions outlined above but found overwhelming majorities who said that candidates' stands and actions on taxes would not influence their vote. Seventy-eight per cent of the respondents expect Dukakis to raise taxes if elected and 69% (including 52% of those intending to vote for him) think Bush will also raise taxes if elected, despite his denials.

Budget deficit: As outlined in Chapter One the deficit has grown enormously during the Reagan years. Public opinion is definitely uneasy about its size, feeling that a legacy has been created which will be a burden to their children. But convincing the majority of people that their taxes need to be raised will not be easy. In their extensive exit polling in the Super Tuesday states on 8 March, CBS asked both Democratic and Republican voters which issues mattered most to them when deciding how to vote on the day. At 36%, 'reducing the federal deficit' was by far the most important reason given by Republican voters. The equivalent response from Democratic voters was 26% – joint second with 'protecting social security benefits' and behind 'unemployment' at 30%. When NBC's own Super Tuesday exit polls asked the direct question, 'Are you worried enough about the federal budget deficit to be willing to have your income taxes increased, or not?', they found, on average, only one-third of Republican voters agreeing and the response of Democratic voters was only a little higher. Perhaps reflecting the fact that the deficit has risen under a Republican administration, when ABC asked respondents in May which candidate would be better at reducing the deficit, 47% chose Dukakis and 35% chose Bush. A July NBC poll on the same question found 42% choosing Dukakis and 29% for Bush.

Education: Education is an issue of increasing concern in the United States, where successive government reports have identified serious problems. In 1983, the National Commission on Excellence in Education entitled their report 'A Nation At Risk' and warned: 'The educational foundations of our society are presently being eroded by a rising tide of mediocrity that threatens our very future.' Five years later, in April 1988, the Education Secretary, William Bennett, published his own report, 'American Education: Making It Work'. Whilst he acknowledged some progress since 1983, he also concluded: 'We are still at risk. The absolute level at which our improvements are taking place is unacceptably low. ... Our students know too little and their command of essential skills is too slight.' Commerce and industry share the concerns of parents and teachers because they see competitive economic growth depending upon better schools and more highly skilled and qualified students. Yet, despite expenditure of nearly $250 billion on elementary, secondary and higher education in 1985, US students consistently performed badly in international comparisons. In addition, confidence in the people running major education institutions, such as colleges and universities, has fallen over the years. A Harris poll in 1966 found 61% of people expressing a great deal of confidence in them: the figure for 1988 was only 34%.

It would seem that education should feature as a major issue in the campaign. Indeed, a National Opinion Research Center survey in 1970 found 49% of people agreeing that too little was being spent on education whereas, by 1987, this had risen to 63%. However, many people view education as essentially a local and state responsibility, with the federal government's role being largely peripheral. As Secretary Bennett wrote in his April report, 'The greatest authority to effect real and lasting change belongs to the state governments, where primary constitutional responsibility for our schools has always rested.'

Drugs: As earlier preoccupations with unemployment and price inflation have subsided, concern about drugs has risen significantly. A CBS/*New York Times* poll in April asked respondents to state what they thought was the most important problem facing the country today. At 16% the rating for drugs was the highest, double the figure for unemployment and for the budget deficit. And this concern runs deep. Americans are not only appalled at the human casualties of drug abuse but also by the corrupting influence of the vast sums of money at the disposal of the drug barons. When a king's ransom is merely small change to those who control the illegal drug trade, the potential for corrupting individuals at every level of American society is almost limitless.

The Reagan administration's initiatives to control and reduce drug abuse were overshadowed by the scandal surrounding General Noriega of Panama earlier this year. At the beginning of June a Harris poll found 63% of respondents agreeing with the statement 'It is shocking to hear that the CIA and other parts of the US government knew about and might even have helped Noriega in his illicit drug activity.' The same poll also found 62% agreeing that the administration had no business offering to drop the grand jury indictment of Noriega if he would give up power and leave Panama. Also in June, an NBC poll found 51% of respondents disapproving of the administration's handling of the situation in Panama (compared with 25% who approved). Such was the mood in the country that NBC found 38% in favour of using American troops to remove Noriega from power (although 46% opposed such action).

By July, 34% of registered voters in an NBC poll thought Dukakis better able to handle the nation's drug problems, compared with a Bush rating of 27% (22% thought neither would make any difference and 17% were not sure).

Health: There is growing concern about the costs to individuals and families of long-term medical care. A Harris poll in February investigated public attitudes in some detail. They found 37% of sampled households reporting that someone in their family now or in the past had needed long-term medical care. There is no real equivalent in the US to the British National Health Service. In the absence of a universal, comprehensive, publicly-funded system of health care much, if not all, of the cost of long-term illness falls upon individuals. Harris found 87% of respondents supporting 'a federal government programme which would help provide for long-term care in the home for elderly people 65 and over who are chronically ill or disabled'. 83% supported similar provision for chronically ill or disabled children aged up to 19.

Another Harris poll, in April, found a decline in public confidence over the years in the medical profession as a whole. In 1966, it achieved the highest confidence rating (73%) among a whole range of institutions (including the White House, the military, the Supreme Court, etc). By 1988, whilst still in the lead, this rating had slumped to 40%.

Harris took an interesting initiative in terms of political polling earlier this year when they amalgamated polls throughout April, May and June and then separately analyzed those respondents who were disabled. They found that the disabled constituted 15% of the adult population and 10% of the electorate. More significantly, they found that 58% of them were intending to vote for Dukakis compared with 34% for Bush (a much wider margin than existed among all other voters).

A majority of Americans are not satisfied with the way the current health system is working and a May Harris poll found Dukakis rated 64% in answer to a question as to which candidate would be best at 'making sure all workers are covered with health insurance provided by their employer', while Bush polled 22%.

Defence: With President Reagan's veto of the $300 billion defence authorization bill on 3 August, the scene was set for one of the major policy debates in the campaign. The President's veto was used because he felt the bill would 'gravely endanger the strategic defense programme' (SDI). Some commentators saw this move as part and parcel of the Republican campaign for November, especially when only hours earlier George Bush had announced his intention, if elected, to 'develop a viable strategic defense system'. Previously Bush had opposed the early deployment of SDI. The Republican strategy will undoubtedly be to portray Dukakis and the Democrats as 'soft' on defence, particularly in the crucial electoral battleground of the South with its long and continuing military tradition. However, there are signs that their task will not be easy.

The view that America needs to have and pay for a strong defence is not in dispute in this election. Where the differences occur is over the level of defence spending. Defence spending has risen from $134 billion in 1980 to an estimated $282 billion in 1987. In real terms (i.e. discounting inflation) this was an increase of 48% over the period. Over the same period, defence expenditure rose from 5% to 6.4% of GNP. The National Opinion Research Center has been monitoring attitudes on the level of defence spending over the years as part of their General Social Surveys. In 1977 they found 26% of people feeling that too little was being spent on 'the military, armaments and defense' compared with 25% who thought America was spending too much. By 1987 these figures had changed to 15% and 42% respectively.

Undoubtedly, defence has become a Republican issue in recent years. A Harris poll of probable voters in June asked which candidate would be best at maintaining a strong defence for the country and found 62% chose Bush compared with 28% for Dukakis. A July NBC poll asked a battery of questions about defence matters. When respondents were asked whether the Reagan administration's build-up of the nation's defences was necessary, 61% answered yes (31% said no). However, when asked to approve the way the administration had managed that same defence build-up, only 49% did so (compared with 41% who disapproved). When asked which candidate was better able to maintain a strong national defence, 49% chose Bush and 30% chose Dukakis.

Soviet Union: As Jon Snow writes in Chapter One, there have been few greater changes in recent history than President Reagan's embrace of Mr Gorbachev and the thawing of US–Soviet relations. But we need to be clear that the attitudes of most Americans towards Communism itself remain steadfastly 'anti'. Early in 1987 the National Opinion Research Center found 56% of respondents describing Communism as 'the worst form of government'. This ought not to be too surprising when we consider the animosity existing between the two superpowers for most of the post-war period. However, shifts in American public opinion have undoubtedly taken place. The Roper organization has asked a set of questions over the years to assess American perceptions about 'Russia's primary objective in world affairs'. Support for the option offering the fiercest anti-Soviet statement ('Russia seeks global domination and will risk a major war to achieve that domination if it can't be achieved by any other means') has fallen from 34% in President Reagan's first year of office, in 1981, to 11% this January. Over the same period, support for the softest statement ('Russia seeks only to protect itself against the possibility of attack by other countries') rose from 6% to 12%.

In January, Market Opinion Research asked whether the Soviet Union could be trusted to keep its part of the agreements in the arms treaty and found 48% saying that they could not, but 43% saying they could. But support for the Senate's ratification of the INF agreement was overwhelming. Also in January, an NBC poll found 67% favouring ratification, including 55% of adults who described themselves as 'very conservative'.

In June, NBC asked respondents whether Dukakis would make a strong leader who could 'stand up to the Russians', or whether he was too inexperienced: 43% declared him a strong leader compared with 39% who thought he was too inexperienced.

Nicaragua and the Contras: Americans are undoubtedly concerned about what they see as the growth of Communism in their own 'backyard'. This is not very surprising given the history of US relations with Castro's Cuba. In March 1986, an ABC poll found 48% agreeing with the statement 'The United States should take all steps including the use of force to prevent the spread of Communism in Central America' (42% disagreed). The significance of the 48% figure rests in the reluctance among Americans, post-Vietnam, to embark on further military engagements in foreign countries. In the following month a CBS poll found 50% agreeing with the statement 'It is important to the security of the United States to eliminate Communism from Latin America'. A further 59% agreed that 'Nicaragua will provide military bases for the Soviet Union'. Only a year earlier (March 1985) a Harris poll found that 60% of respondents agreed that 'The Sandinista government in Nicaragua will become another Communist outpost like Cuba unless the US puts real pressure on them to either change radically or be overthrown'. By March 1987, ABC News still found 56% of Americans who regarded the situation in Nicaragua as 'a threat to the security of the United States'.

However, as Jon Snow comments in Chapter One, US aid to the Contra rebels fighting the Sandinista government has consistently met with a large degree of public opposition. In August 1987, an ABC poll found 59% opposing military and other aid to the Contras, compared with 36% who favoured such aid.

Israel and the Middle East: Israel's handling of Palestinian unrest on the West Bank and in Gaza this year has caused some damage to her standing in the US but this seems unlikely to be permanent. A Harris poll in late January found 60% of Americans agreeing that Israeli troops were wrong to use real rather than rubber bullets to stop the disorders. In early February a Gallup poll found 30% of respondents viewing Israel less favourably as a result of the anti-riot measures (61% said their views remain unchanged). But, whilst traditional American support remains strong, there is also a desire to see a negotiated settlement to the continuing dispute, including direct talks between the US and the PLO.

South Africa: The issue of South Africa has come into particular focus this year with the decision by the Democrats to declare it a 'terrorist state' if they win the White House. In May 1987 Gallup found 63% of adults expressing various degrees of unfavourable opinion about South Africa. In August 1987 Media General found 49% supporting the proposition that US companies should stop doing business in South Africa (34% opposed). And, in July 1987, the Roper organization tried to discover whether the American public thought US business investments ultimately helped or hurt the black population of South Africa. Roper had asked the same questions in February 1985. In 1987, the number who felt that investment helped the blacks amounted to 24% (only 1% less than in 1985). However, the number who felt that investment hurt black South Africans had risen from 21% in 1985 to 31% in 1987 (the remainder were made up of people who said they had not followed the issue closely enough or did not know).

Overall, Dukakis has led in the polls on most domestic issues for much of 1988. George Bush has led on defence and on the general question of experience in handling foreign affairs. Public opinion may well shift across a whole range of these issues as the campaign moves into top gear – not least as a result of each candidate seeking to mount raids into the other's 'territory'.

CHAPTER THREE

The Rules of the Game

QUALIFICATIONS FOR THE PRESIDENCY

The Constitution of the United States lays down the formal qualifications for the presidency. A president must be at least 35 years old, born an American citizen and have been resident in the United States for at least 14 years. No person can be elected to the office more than twice and no one who has served more than two years of a term to which another president was elected can be elected in his own right more than once.

The formal rules only tell part of the story, however. Arguably, the only national purpose which exists in American politics is the election of the sole national official – the President. The reality of modern American politics is that a presidential candidate must be the nominee of either the Republican or Democratic parties in order to secure a broad coalitional base for the assembly of a majority. Third-party bids for the presidency like John Anderson's in 1980 or George Wallace's in 1968 have a long history of failure.

To gain the nomination a candidate has to have a significant political record. The parties and the electorate will only normally consider someone who has previously been a congressman, senator or governor. Talk of outsider candidacies by men such as the industrialist Lee Iacocca has not usually come to much. The election of Dwight Eisenhower was an exception. His wartime record allowed him to avoid the normal apprenticeship. Of the eight post-war presidents, seven had previously held high political office. Two were former governors, four former vice-presidents, and four former senators. Truman, Johnson, Nixon, and Ford, the former vice-presidents, had also all served in Congress. The last and only person to be elected directly to the presidency from the House of Representatives was James A. Garfield of Ohio in 1881. After an undistinguished career of 18 years as a Republican congressman, he was nominated on the 36th ballot. Even Garfield was, at the time of his election, a US senator-elect, but was still a sitting congressman. He won the presidency by 0.02% of the popular vote and was shot shortly after his inauguration. Not a particularly happy precedent for subsequent attempts by House members – Richard Gephardt's candidacy for the Democratic nomination this year is the most recent instance of failure.

Until now all American presidents have been white and male. But Americans still seem to have faith in the ability of the system to allow someone to rise from the 'log cabin' to the White House. A poll in June this year showed that 59% of Americans thought it possible for their child to become president.

THE ELECTORAL COLLEGE

Although 8 November is election day the new president will not strictly speaking be elected on that day. American presidential elections are not contests for the popular vote but for a majority in the electoral college.

In each state voters cast their ballots for a slate of electors pledged to support a presidential candidate. Normally a candidate who wins a majority of the popular vote in a state takes all its electoral college votes.

Each state has a fixed number of electors equal to the number of people it sends to Congress (its representatives plus its two senators). Therefore California, the most populous state, which has 45 congressmen and two senators has 47 electors. Wyoming with a tiny population has just one congressman and two senators, and so has three electoral college votes. In 1964 the 23rd Amendment to the Constitution gave three electoral votes to the District of Columbia, making the total in the electoral college 538. That is the equivalent of the 100 senators, 435 congressmen and three votes from Washington DC. So, 270 electoral college votes are needed to win the presidency.

The Electoral College as a whole does not meet in one place. Instead the electors meet in their respective state capitals on the first Monday after the second Wednesday in December. This year that will be 19 December.

The Electoral College was instituted because the Founding Fathers distrusted direct democracy and wanted to give the small states more influence than they would otherwise have. Over the last 100 years the college has simply confirmed the result of the national vote. But on three occasions in the past – 1824 (John Adams), 1876 (Rutherford Hayes) and 1888 (Benjamin Harrison) – it elected presidents who had won fewer votes than their opponents in the popular ballot. If this year is a close election the same could happen again.

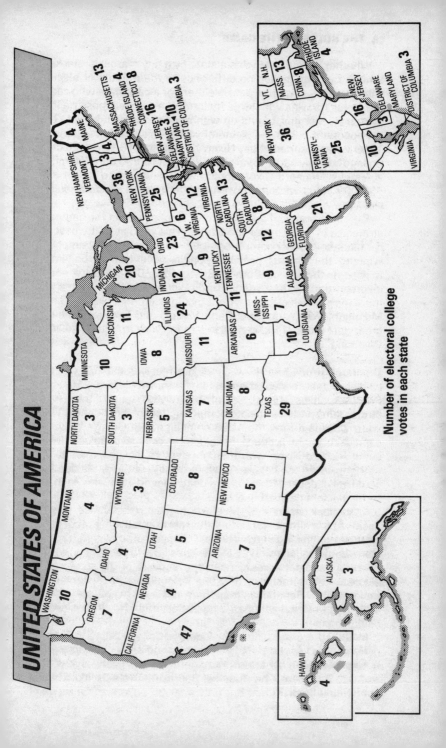

UNITED STATES OF AMERICA

Number of electoral college votes in each state

WASHINGTON 10
OREGON 7
CALIFORNIA 47
NEVADA 4
IDAHO 4
UTAH 5
ARIZONA 7
MONTANA 4
WYOMING 3
COLORADO 8
NEW MEXICO 5
NORTH DAKOTA 3
SOUTH DAKOTA 3
NEBRASKA 5
KANSAS 7
OKLAHOMA 8
TEXAS 29
MINNESOTA 10
IOWA 8
MISSOURI 11
ARKANSAS 6
LOUISIANA 10
WISCONSIN 11
ILLINOIS 24
MICHIGAN 20
INDIANA 12
OHIO 23
KENTUCKY 9
TENNESSEE 11
MISSISSIPPI 7
ALABAMA 9
GEORGIA 12
FLORIDA 21
SOUTH CAROLINA 8
NORTH CAROLINA 13
VIRGINIA 12
W. VIRGINIA 6
PENNSYLVANIA 25
NEW YORK 36
MAINE 4
NEW HAMPSHIRE 4
VERMONT 3
MASSACHUSETTS 13
RHODE ISLAND 4
CONNECTICUT 8
NEW JERSEY 16
DELAWARE 3
MARYLAND 10
DISTRICT OF COLUMBIA 3
ALASKA 3
HAWAII 4

Inset

NEW YORK 36
PENNSYLVANIA 25
VIRGINIA 10
VT. N.H.
MASS. 13
CONN. 8
RHODE ISLAND 4
NEW JERSEY 16
DELAWARE 3
MARYLAND 10
DISTRICT OF COLUMBIA 3

Whether a candidate wins a state by a tiny margin or stacks up a huge majority makes no difference to the number of electoral votes he wins. It is quite possible then for a candidate who carries the states he wins with large majorities, and loses those he loses by narrow margins, to end up with more of the popular vote than his opponent but fewer electoral votes. This nearly happened in 1960 when Kennedy beat Nixon by 303 to 219 in the Electoral College but only had a popular majority of 118,550 out of 60 million votes cast. Richard Nixon could easily have picked up an extra 150,000 votes without converting that into an electoral college victory.

The main practical influence of the college is on the campaign strategies of presidential candidates. This year, as in the past, the candidates are concentrating their campaigns not simply on winning the biggest possible popular vote but on building a majority in the college. Both Mr Bush and Mr Dukakis are spending disproportionate time, money and resources in those states with more than fifteen electors. The voters in California, Florida, Illinois, Michigan, New York, Ohio, Pennsylvania and Texas are seeing a great deal more of the candidates than those in South Dakota or Wyoming.

Deadlock procedure: If no candidate receives the 270 electoral college votes needed, the election is thrown into the House of Representatives. This would only be likely to happen if there was a strong third-party candidate competing for the presidency. There were worries during the 1968 campaign that George Wallace's candidacy might produce an electoral college deadlock. In the event Richard Nixon won enough electoral college votes to win outright. In a race between just two major candidates deadlock could only happen if there was a dead heat on 269 votes each or if some electors decided to abstain.

If deadlock occurs and the election goes to the House, it is not decided by a simple vote of all the representatives. Rather, each state delegation is given one vote. The representatives within each state would ballot amongst themselves how to cast that vote. The winning candidate would need the support of 26 states to be elected. At the moment 31 state delegations have Democratic majorities, 10 Republican majorities and 9 are evenly split. But all 435 congressional seats are up for election in November, so that could change.

In 1800 there was a tie in the Electoral College between Thomas Jefferson and Aaron Burr. They were standing on the same ticket but had not been separately nominated for the posts of president and vice-president. The House of Representatives decided Jefferson should be president but only after 36 ballots and a week of voting. To stop this happening again the 12th Amendment to the Constitution was passed in 1804. It provided for separate ballots for the two offices.

VOTER REGISTRATION AND TURNOUT

The United States has one of the worst records of voter participation among Western industrialized democracies. In 1984 the Harvard/ABC News Symposium produced a league table of voter turnout for 24 countries, listing their most recent major national elections as of 1983 (voting in Australia, Belgium and Italy is, by law, compulsory). The US turnout is based on the voting-age population and for all others upon registered voters.

Voter turnout

	%			%
1. Belgium	95	13.	Denmark	83
2. Australia	94	14.	Norway	82
3. Austria	92	15.	Greece	79
4. Sweden	91	16.	Israel	78
5. Italy	90	17.	United Kingdom	76
6. Iceland	89	18.	Japan	74
7. New Zealand	89	19.	Canada	69
8. Luxembourg	89	20.	Spain	68
9. West Germany	87	21.	Finland	64
10. Netherlands	87	22.	Ireland	62
11. France	86	23.	United States	53
12. Portugal	84	24.	Switzerland	48

Looking at turnout amongst *registered* voters in the US the Symposium found a significant change in the table. At 87% the United States rose to eleventh position.

However, interest and debate concentrates upon the fact that, on 8 November, tens of millions of US citizens, aged 18 plus, will simply not be eligible to vote for the next President of their country because they are not registered. In January, the independent Committee for the Study of the American Electorate, reported on voter participation and registration. They commented:

> The United States stands alone among the world's democracies in making voting a two-step act, requiring the citizen to register prior to voting. In every other advanced democracy, the state (in whole or in part) establishes the voting list. In most, all the citizen has to do is vote.

Clearly, in other countries the citizen is obliged to complete the registration form, but the point is that the government authorities are responsible for sending it (which is *not* the case in the United

States). In the US the onus for registration rests entirely upon the individual citizen.

In their more polemical work *Why Americans Don't Vote* (Pantheon Books, New York 1988), Piven and Cloward offer more trenchant criticism:

> American registration procedures are Byzantine compared with those that prevail in other democracies. ... The United States is the only major democracy where government assumes no responsibility for helping citizens cope with voter registration procedures. In 1980, 39 to 40 per cent of the American electorate was unregistered, or more than 60 million in an eligible voting-age population of 159 million, and two out of three of the unregistered resided in households with incomes below the median.

Voting qualifications differ from state to state because Article 1, Section 2 of the US Constitution permits them to set their own voting standards (although the Constitution also lays down broad guarantees). Those wishing to vote have to register themselves with their local authority by a set time in the year and in compliance with the particular arrangements operated by their state. Only after initiating and then successfully completing this operation are their names placed on the electoral roll which enables them to vote. A handful of states allow voters to register on election day itself and half allow registration by post. Turnout by state varies significantly:

% of voting-age population voting in the 1984 presidential election

	%		%
Minnesota	68.5	Louisiana	54.2
Maine	65.2	New Hampshire	53.9
Montana	65.0	Pennsylvania	53.9
South Dakota	63.8	Arkansas	52.2
Wisconsin	63.4	Mississippi	52.0
North Dakota	62.9	Wyoming	51.8
Oregon	62.6	New Mexico	51.6
Iowa	62.3	Maryland	51.4
Connecticut	61.0	West Virginia	51.3
Utah	60.5	Oklahoma	51.2
Idaho	60.4	New York	51.1
Alaska	60.2	Virginia	51.1
Vermont	60.0	Kentucky	50.7
Washington	58.5	Alabama	50.2
Michigan	58.2	California	49.9
Ohio	58.2	Tennessee	49.3
Massachusetts	57.9	Florida	49.0
Missouri	57.7	North Carolina	47.7
Illinois	57.3	Texas	47.0

Kansas	57.0	Arizona	46.6
New Jersey	56.9	Hawaii	44.5
Indiana	56.3	Dist. of Columbia	43.8
Nebraska	56.1	Georgia	42.2
Rhode Island	56.0	Nevada	41.6
Delaware	55.7	South Carolina	40.6
Colorado	54.8		

A gap of almost 28% between the highest turnout in Minnesota and the lowest in South Carolina requires some explanation. In part low turnout is due to higher mobility in some states. Also, it partly reflects the degree of restriction which individual states place on voter registration.

One could offer the Theory of the 37th Parallel: above it there are 35 mainland states (excluding Alaska and Hawaii) containing the ten highest turnouts. Only two – California and Nevada (both intersected by the 37th Parallel) – have turnouts lower than 50% (49.9% and 41.6% respectively). Below that line there are 13 states which account for seven of the lowest ten turnouts in the country.

Throughout the history of the United States there have been no fewer than five amendments to the Constitution designed either to widen the franchise or circumvent attempts by individual states to deny the vote to specific groups. The 14th Amendment (1868) instructed Congress to reduce the representation from any state which denied the vote to any adult male other than criminals (no reduction was ever made). The 15th Amendment (1870) sought to prohibit the disenfranchisement of any citizen 'on account of race, colour or previous condition of servitude'. However, in response, a number of states immediately set about erecting a whole battery of measures to thwart the enfranchisement of blacks, including literacy tests, poll tax qualifications and elaborate registration requirements. Women were allowed the vote as a result of the 19th Amendment (1920) which prohibited denial of the franchise 'on account of sex'. The 24th Amendment (adopted in 1964) declared that 'the right of citizens of the United States to vote in any [federal elections] shall not be denied or abridged by the United States or any state by reason of failure to pay any poll tax or any other tax'. (Two years later the Supreme Court applied the same principle to state elections. Justice Douglas, speaking for the majority, stated that 'wealth or fee paying has, in our view, no relation to voting qualifications; the right to vote is too precious, too fundamental, to be so burdened or conditioned'.) The 26th Amendment (1971) lowered the voting age to 18. In addition, the 23rd Amendment (1961) gave the right to vote in presidential elections to the population of the District of Columbia.

A further weapon in the armoury of measures to combat

discrimination against voters was the 1965 Voting Rights Act. This measure strictly limited the power of the states to determine who could register and vote, as well as introducing a degree of federal supervision. Section 2 of the Act stated that '[no] voting qualification or prerequisite to vote or standard, practice, or procedure shall be imposed or applied … in a manner which results in a denial or abridgement of the right of any citizen of the United States to vote on account of race or colour'. Amendments were made to the Act, in 1982, which strengthened its provisions, most particularly by introducing a new standard for proving violations. As a result aspiring voters no longer have to prove that their state's electoral procedures are *intended* to be discriminatory, but simply that they *result* in discrimination. The amendments ensured that the electoral procedures covered 'include all action necessary to make a vote effective in any primary, special or general election, including, but not limited to, registration'.

Nationwide turnout in presidential elections: 1944–84

	%
1944	56
1948	51
1952	62
1956	59
1960	63
1964	62
1968	61
1972	55
1976	54
1980	53
1984	53

(Source: US Bureau of the Census)

The figures above are based on the turnout of the voting-age population in each election year. It will be seen that turnout since 1944 peaked in 1960 and has declined steadily since then. However, turnout is significantly lower in nationwide elections when there is no presidential contest. In the most recent, in 1986, turnout was 33.4% of the voting-age population – considerably less than the turnout in Britain's local government elections that same year.

This year there are about 180 million people of voting age in the United States, out of a population of 243 million. One estimate suggests that between 90 and 95 million people are likely to vote on 8 November. If so, there is no prospect of any dramatic reversal of the declining turnout of recent years.

Certainly the profile of the non-voter seems to have changed in recent years. In the July/August issue of the US journal *Public Opinion*, Ruy Teixeira gave an account of those changes:

> In 1960, 72% of nonvoters had less than a high school education; by 1980 this figure had dropped to 39%. Similarly, in 1960, 60% of nonvoters were poor (less than $5,000 family income in 1960 dollars), whereas in 1980 only 44% were poor (using the same criterion). About 7% of nonvoters were under age twenty-five in 1960, while in 1980, 25% were under age twenty-five. Thirty-seven percent were mobile and 26% were single in 1960; by 1980 each of these categories captured half of the nonvoting population.

A variety of explanations for the declining voter participation have been volunteered. The report of the Panel on the Electoral and Democratic Process of the President's Commission for a National Agenda for the Eighties (set up by President Carter), looking at falling turnout, declared: 'This growing public alienation surely reflects an outlook among citizens that our political institutions have not responded adequately to the welter of troublesome problems confronting our nation.'

Piven and Cloward see the decline as a result of the creation of obstacles to the franchise rather than of voter apathy:

> Elites are confirmed structuralists. If that were not so, they would have long since acquiesced to the universal registration of American citizens in the sure confidence that nothing would change. Whether an enlarged electorate would transform American politics can only be known, finally, by obliterating the remaining obstacles to voting.

Other commentators point to less sinister explanations: the modern dominance of television which is felt to make contests far more impersonal than in the past; the decline of political parties and therefore of their ability to mobilize voters; disillusionment with the competence of government and the quality of candidates for elected office; growing scepticism about whether the whole political process (and, therefore, voting itself) has any effect upon the daily life of the average citizen; and, indeed, the very profusion of elections themselves.

However, there is clearly a persistent worry that the low level of voter participation cannot be good for American democracy.

CAMPAIGN FINANCING

Money is almost essential for success in American presidential politics these days. Abraham Lincoln spent about $100,000 on his 1860 campaign, but Richard Nixon's second campaign in 1972 cost some $60 million. Precise figures are impossible to establish because it is often difficult in a presidential election year to distinguish between what is spent on the presidential race itself and what parties spend on Senate, House, gubernatorial and local elections. Estimates of what unpaid labour is worth are not included in candidates' accounts.

The law used to play no part in restricting the amounts spent or the sources of financial contributions. Traditionally, reforming candidates were at a considerable disadvantage to those favouring big business, or even, in the case of progressively minded politicians like Woodrow Wilson, found themselves having to accept monies from the very interests they were attacking.

There have been several serious attempts at dealing with the problem of unrestricted financial contributions, the first being the Hatch Act of 1939. This laid down that no one could give more than $5,000 to a presidential candidate in any single year and also restricted each political group to spending no more than $3 million on a presidential campaign. The Act, however, proved ineffective in achieving its aims, and further proposed reforms came to nothing.

In 1970 President Nixon vetoed a bill that would have limited what could be spent on television advertising. However, Congress still felt that there was a need for legislation and in 1971 passed the Federal Election Campaign Act (FECA). After the excesses of the Republican's 1972 campaign and in particular the activities of the Committee to Re-elect the President which culminated in the Watergate scandal, it was felt still tougher legislation was required.

Amendments were duly made to the FECA in 1974, 1976 and 1979 and these provide the basis for the current financial rules. These laws were designed to encourage small contributions from individuals (up to a maximum of $1,000) and discourage 'fat cat' donors. Federal matching funds were introduced for candidates who could raise at least $5,000 from each of 20 states in individual donations of less than $250. For each dollar the candidate raises he gets a dollar from the public purse. And the public purse is literally filled by the public. Since 1972, all US citizens have been able to indicate on their tax returns whether or not $1 of their taxes should go to the Presidential Election Campaign Fund (first used in 1976). About one-quarter of US taxpayers contribute to the Fund.

Money contributed by Political Action Committees (PACs) does not qualify for matching funds. There are over 4,000 PACs in operation and they generally represent business, trade union and professional associations which want to donate money to candidates who support their causes and special interests. Each PAC may contribute a maximum of $5,000 per candidate in each campaign. Most of them originate in the business sector and therefore generally favour the Republicans.

There is no obligation to accept federal funding and candidates who do not accept it may spend unlimited amounts of money (although contributions from PACs and individuals are still subject to the limits of $5,000 and $1,000 respectively). However, if candidates, both in the nomination race and in the presidential election itself, accept federal financial support then they have also to accept set limits on their total spending. In the nomination races these are set for each individual state and in the presidential election there is a national limit.

The overall limit this year for the nomination races in all the states combined was about $22 million. Individual state spending limits are set on the basis of the voting-age population. So, states with small populations, such as Alaska, Wyoming and Vermont had limits of $444,000 for each candidate whilst the limit for California was $7 million and for New York, nearly $5 million. The Democratic and Republican National Committees also receive public funds to help finance their National Conventions. Any third-party or independent candidate (such as John Anderson in 1980) must win more than 5% of the overall vote in a presidential election to qualify for federal funds – payable after the campaign.

It is estimated that this year taxpayers will have contributed $64 million to all the presidential candidates in the nomination races. In the presidential election itself the taxpayer picks up most of the bill. The Presidential Election Campaign Fund Act of 1971 states that, as a condition of receiving public funding, the 'candidates and their authorized committees will not incur qualified campaign expenses in excess of the aggregate payments to which they will be entitled' which this year should amount to about $47 million for each of the two candidates. The Act also requires that 'no contributions to defray qualified campaign expenses have been or will be accepted by such candidates or any of their authorized committees'. Two exceptions are allowed: firstly, if the Fund does not contain enough money to meet the limit per candidate then each can seek funds to take them up to the limit; and, secondly, it allows for a formula to divide expenditure where money is used both to elect presidential candidates and candidates for other federal, state or local office. In addition to that the parties can spend $8 million on their nominees and unlimited amounts actually getting the vote out on 8 November.

The advent of federal funding has had an impact on the nature of campaigning itself. To gain maximum benefit campaign planning needs to start earlier; direct mail appeals are more important than ever; and lawyers, accountants and computer specialists have become key personnel in any headquarters' staff.

THE INFLUENCE OF TELEVISION

One of the main reasons for the high cost of presidential campaigns is the increasing influence of television: campaigns spend, on average, around two-thirds of the money available to them on television advertising. But the rest, which is spent on travel and direct campaigning, is just as important in attracting the attention of television viewers.

The days of 'whistle stop' tours, when presidential candidates campaigned from the backs of trains in hundreds of small communities across America, are long gone. Modern campaigning is essentially campaigning by television (radio was first used in the 1924 presidential election, and television first made its mark in the 1952 campaign). In 1950 only 4,400,000 American homes had television sets. Ten years later that figure had multiplied tenfold to 45 million. By the early 1980s, 80 million homes had at least one television set, and many had more than one: 98% of the population now have access to a television set. Television has become the main means by which most Americans receive their news. Politics has adapted to the change.

Modern campaign travel schedules are designed almost entirely to draw the television networks into covering the candidate and the message. The evening news bulletins of the four national networks ABC, NBC, CBS and the newer 24-hour Cable News Network are where the campaign strategists want to deliver their pitch.

In the old days, when television used film rather than video tape and reports were flown into New York rather than relayed by satellite, candidates had to make their main points in the morning to get them on the nightly news. Now television news is an instant medium. A speech recorded in the morning will be old news by 7 pm and opposing candidates will have had plenty of time to respond, so the campaigns try to make important announcements early enough to catch the network deadlines, but too late to allow opponents any comeback. Campaigning for the White House has become in large part a game of grand strategy played by television professionals.

Television's role is especially important in the early days of a presidential election year. When there are a large number of candidates, most of whom are not well known beyond their own states, television news often determines which candidates are taken seriously and which are not. This is especially true on primary election nights, when the networks compete with each other to spot 'winners' and 'losers' based on small numbers of votes. In 1976 the relatively unknown Jimmy Carter was given a massive boost when the networks declared him the undisputed winner in the Iowa caucuses. There had been a small turnout and

Carter got just 29% of the vote, less than the 39% that went to uncommitted delegates. Nevertheless the networks declared him the winner and gave him all-important momentum going into New Hampshire. In this year's primary season, following his humiliation in Iowa, George Bush used television advertising to turn the tide in his favour in New Hampshire.

The great set pieces of the election campaign itself are the televised debates between the candidates: two men locked in combat where the weapons are image and the telling remark. Pollsters say they shift more swing votes than any other feature of a campaign. The debates which are nowadays seen as an essential part of every election only started in 1960 with the contest between Kennedy and Nixon. Before the debates, Kennedy had been portrayed by the Republicans as a rich and immature candidate who had won the nomination with his father's money and influence. On television Kennedy proved himself to be easily Nixon's equal. Nixon, who declined to use stage make-up, looked shifty and sweated profusely. The viewers decided Kennedy had won. The election turned out to be close and the debates were seen as having played a crucial part in determining the result.

In 1964 Lyndon Johnson declined to debate with Goldwater and in 1968 and 1972 Nixon, remembering the experience of 1960, also decided not to participate. They had a legal excuse. The law stated that all candidates must be given equal access to television air time unless Congress suspended the regulation (minority party candidates could argue that debates between the major party candidates infringed their right of equal access). Congress had suspended the rules in 1960 but was not keen to do so again. In 1976 however the networks found a way around the problem. The League of Women Voters was encouraged to stage debates and the networks covered them as news events. Since then no candidate has had the opportunity to back out. The League decides the locations and the rules for the debates.

Half the American population watches the debates. In 1980 Reagan was generally thought to have won the contests and surged ahead in the polls. In 1984 Mondale did better but not well enough to cut Reagan's already enormous lead significantly. If this year's election is as close as 1960 the debates could again be seen as the crucial factor in determining the outcome.

Ronald Reagan is regarded as the classic example of the modern television candidate. His first foray into politics came in 1964, when he made television commercials in support of Barry Goldwater's presidential campaign. The campaign was a failure, but the commercials were considered a success. Reagan went on to use television more effectively than any other politician, first in California and then nationally. His election to the presidency in

1980 and re-election in 1984 were seen as the triumph of the televisually packaged candidate, the victory of the great communicator. He had succeeded in doing with television what Roosevelt had accomplished with radio. But if the lesson of the early 1980s was that the best television performer would rise to the top, then this year's events may force commentators to think again.

Neither party has chosen a natural television performer as candidate. Michael Dukakis, who, ironically, chaired a television discussion programme in the 1970s, does not perform easily on the medium. Critics say his 'body language' makes him seem ill at ease. But Mr Bush's performances this year have been even poorer. One in particular stands out.

In early June he was interviewed on ABC's Nightline by Ted Koppel. Bush's mind seemed to wander and on several occasions he called the interviewer Dan, an apparent reference to CBS's Dan Rather with whom he had had a memorable argument during the primary campaign. Several times Koppel reminded Bush that his name was Ted. At one point the Vice-President said, 'Did I do it again? Hey, listen, it's Freudian. I am not trying to be clever. I promise you it's Freudian.' The name was not the only problem. Throughout the interview the Vice-President came across as evasive and not in command of the facts. He meandered through answers and said he could not remember important details on matters such as Panama because he did not have his notes to hand. The performance reminded some commentators of television events that have sunk previous presidential campaigns. They pointed to the Edward Kennedy interview with Roger Mudd in which he couldn't find the words to explain why he wanted to be President, and to the 1960 debates discussed above. The Koppel interview probably was not as damaging but it did give the critics and the cartoonists further ammunition against Bush.

The fact that the men who have emerged as the nominees of the major parties are not naturally good at performing on television could suggest that its role in sorting out candidates has been exaggerated. But equally it can be said that there were even poorer television performers who lost in the primaries. Bruce Babbitt, the darling of the newspaper journalists, always appeared dull on the small screen. This may be one reason why his campaign did not survive beyond New Hampshire.

Television does not create presidents. But it is, and will for the forseeable future remain, the most important medium for campaigning and the electorate's main source of information on the choice before it. No candidate, however instinctively antagonistic towards the medium, can ignore that.

CHAPTER FOUR

The Road to the Conventions

INTRODUCTION

'The basic characteristic of US primaries is: "shoot the wounded".'
(Richard Scammon)

What is a Primary? The presidential primary is one of the most distinctive features of the US electoral system . Its essential purpose is to elect delegates to the parties' National Conventions, where the presidential nominees are chosen. It developed out of the great reform movement at the turn of the century, where progressives, populists and reformers campaigned against state and municipal corruption – particularly the close links between political bosses and big business. Part of this fight was to break the boss-dominated party conventions by instituting primary elections through which the voters of the party could have a part in choosing the presidential candidate. Florida, in 1901, was the first state to introduce a law enacting a presidential primary system. By 1912, 12 states had adopted legislation requiring presidential primaries that provided for either direct election of delegates, a vote for candidates, or both. By 1916 this number had grown to 26.

However, the old party system proved more resilient than the reformers expected. In 1912, the Republican convention chose a candidate who won only one out of twelve primaries, and in 1916 and 1920, the Republican candidates who were nominated both performed badly in the primaries. Interest waned and by 1935 eight states had repealed their presidential primary laws.

Post-1945, interest increased again as candidates, not favoured by their party establishments, entered primaries to demonstrate their attractiveness to voters and their organizational abilities, and in order to generate a bandwagon effect. In the 1960s and early 1970s the presidential primaries become more popular as a route to nomination. By 1976, 26 states and the District of Columbia held primaries; this year the Democrats held primaries in 34 states and the Republicans in 36, as well as in the District of Columbia and territories such as Puerto Rico.

As the number of state primaries has grown, the importance of the earlier ones has increased. Candidates seek to create early bandwagons to attract media interest and financial support which assists them in the later primaries. The Carter campaign in 1976 hardly looked back when he won four out of the first five state primaries. Conversely, in 1984 Walter Mondale, although finally winning the nomination, never recovered from the damage inflicted on him by Gary Hart's successes (Hart won five out of the first seven primaries).

It has been argued in recent years that the role of the primary is changing. With the campaign season having grown so long, and the profusion of opinion polls registering support for individual candidates, some people see the primaries now as endorsing the result rather than opening out the selection process. Certainly, the existing system has never been without its critics. Since 1911, hundreds of bills have been introduced in Congress to reform the system, but all have floundered. Proposals have been made more recently to create a single, nationwide primary; to create regional primaries (where individual states within a geographical region would hold their primaries on the same day); and to standardize the dates of primaries to shorten the campaign season.

The parties employ a mixture of proportional representation primaries and winner-take-all primaries. Most Democratic delegates at their convention are divided proportionately on the basis of primary results with candidates needing just 15% of the vote to qualify for a share of the delegates. The Republicans operate a mix of proportional and winner-take-all primaries.

Another variation is that between open and closed primaries. States that do require registration by party have closed primaries in which voters vote according to party registration. In closed primaries, independents are precluded and no crossovers are allowed. Anyone can vote in open primaries.

The essential fact is that this year over 35 million voters have presented themselves at local polling stations to vote for the candidate of their choice either directly or by voting for delegates who will support him. It is the votes of these many millions of people which have effectively decided who should be the nominees of the two main parties in November, rather than a handful of party bosses in concert with small groups of vested interests.

Throughout this chapter we have concentrated upon primaries because they generate significantly larger turnouts and attention these days. Caucuses are overwhelmingly restricted to small states (of the large states, only Michigan this year held a caucus rather than a primary). The Iowa caucus is the regular exception because, by state law, it has always to be the first contest of the primary/caucus season and therefore candidates invest a great deal of time and money there.

For all the criticism of the length of the primary campaign many believe there really is no alternative. One of this year's early casualties, Democrat Bruce Babbitt, wrote reflectively in the *Guardian* in March:

> The process is long and arduous and I've spent my share of lonely nights in motels in small midwestern towns wondering whether there's a better way. But I'm not sure there is. For all its defects, the system does have a certain logic, and I would not advocate basic change.
>
> Those who say American presidential campaigns last too long point to England, where equivalent campaigns last just six to eight weeks. But the United States doesn't have a parliamentary system in which the party candidates are in place years ahead of the election. We generate our national leadership, in part, from among our most successful regional leaders, not all of whom are well known to the nation at large. America is a huge, continental nation. Candidates and voters need time to get acquainted. Better too much time than too little.

What is a Caucus? 'Caucus' comes from an Indian word meaning 'to gather together and make a big noise'. It came to be used to describe the eighteenth-century system of town and village meetings that were held in New England both to select candidates for office and conduct other political business. During the first four decades of the United States, all presidential candidates were chosen by the caucus system.

The caucus method of delegate selection varies from state to state. In states such as Iowa, citizens gather at informal, neighbourhood-level meetings of Democratic and Republican voters, and stand in groups to publicly announce support for a candidate. These meetings select delegates to go to county conventions and from there to district or state conventions where the national convention delegates are selected.

Elections take place over roughly the same period as the primaries, but the selection process is longer, sometimes taking a month to complete. Popular participation is only at the first – precinct – level.

THE DEMOCRATS

Many months of preparation, endless miles of footslogging and countless handshakes all came to a head in the Iowa caucus on 8 February which marked the opening of the Democratic candidate race. The leading contenders at this stage included Bruce Babbitt, former Governor of Arizona; Michael Dukakis, Governor of Massachusetts; Richard Gephardt, Congressman for Missouri; Albert Gore, Senator for Tennessee; Gary Hart, former Senator for Colorado; the Revd Jesse Jackson; and Paul Simon, Senator for Illinois.

Before scandal forced him out of the race in May 1987, Gary Hart dominated the polls in Iowa even though he had come a very poor second to Walter Mondale there in 1984. Following his departure Paul Simon took the lead, followed by Michael Dukakis and Richard Gephardt. Hart's re-entry into the race threw a live grenade into the proceedings and, for a brief moment, he again became the leading contender (although by a much smaller margin than before).

But Hart's support evaporated almost as quickly as it had been rekindled. It was Richard Gephardt who won the laurels on the day. He had persistently backed protectionist legislation in the House of Representatives and in Iowa this became his principal theme. He gambled heavily by spending $500,000 on television advertisements which aggressively spelt out his protectionist message. The money was well spent: he secured 31% of the votes with Simon coming second with 27% and Dukakis third with 22%. Largely buried in the news surrounding the victor was the significant 9% registered for Jesse Jackson, in a state where blacks comprise only 1% of the population and where he secured only 1.5% of the 1984 primary vote.

The Democratic contest in New Hampshire, the first primary of the campaign, lacked the tense excitement of the Republican race. Michael Dukakis had held a dominant lead in the state polls for many months and won the vote comfortably with a 16% lead over Gephardt and with Simon narrowly in third place. Jesse Jackson again improved on his 1984 performance but Gary Hart, who won the state handsomely in 1984, finished bottom of the poll with a mere 4% of the vote. Although less bitter than the Republican contest, this first primary nevertheless marked an outbreak of hostilities between some of the Democratic candidates. Paul Simon had used television commercials to stress how Gephardt's campaign statements differed from his voting record in Congress and claimed that he could not be trusted. Both declared that they had performed well enough to continue in the race but doubts were expressed about whether Simon could raise sufficient funds to remain for long.

Only seven days later, on 23 February, the candidates faced a primary in South Dakota (technically non-binding although delegates were likely to be distributed according to their share of the vote) and a caucus in Minnesota. Gephardt had concentrated nearly all his effort on South Dakota (he trailed in fifth in Minnesota) and won by a margin of 12% over Dukakis. Dukakis in turn won in Minnesota but Gephardt could take comfort in the fact that 32% of the voting-age population of South Dakota participated in its state primaries, compared with the 5% who participated in the Minnesota caucuses. Paul Simon was the real loser from these results. Earlier he had hinted that he would have to win either state if he was to stay in the race. His effort was now chronically divided between campaigning and taking time off to raise funds to continue. Indeed, he had to announce that he would 'sit out' Super Tuesday. Doubtless, he hoped to cling on until Illinois, his home state, held its primary immediately after. Jesse Jackson scored nearly 20% of the votes in Minnesota, polling strongly in some predominantly white areas. Gary Hart secured his best vote so far with 6% in South Dakota but captured less than 1% in Minnesota.

On 28 February just under 9,000 voters participated in the Maine caucus which Michael Dukakis won. Now, only Vermont stood between the candidates and the primaries on Super Tuesday. The Vermont primary, on 1 March, was won comfortably by Michael Dukakis (although Jesse Jackson continued his remarkable run by securing 26% of the votes and second place).

Super Tuesday: Sixteen states held primaries on Tuesday 7 March – hence the title 'Super Tuesday'. This unprecedented concentration was the product of a strategy by southern Democrats. They judged that such a raft of southern primaries on the same day would have two effects: firstly, to promote the nomination of a moderate Democratic candidate, electable in the South; and, secondly, to create a bandwagon of southern voter participation in Democratic contests which would, hopefully, carry through and translate into Democratic votes on 8 November. The outcome suggested that they were not particularly successful in either aim.

The result for the Democrats was indecisive. In summary: Jesse Jackson won five states (Alabama, Georgia, Louisiana, Mississippi and Virginia); Albert Gore won another five (Arkansas, Kentucky, North Carolina, Oklahoma and his home state of Tennessee); Michael Dukakis also won five (Florida, Maryland, his home state of Massachusetts, Rhode Island and Texas); and Richard Gephardt won only his home state of Missouri. Far from reducing the Democratic field, Super Tuesday gave varying degrees of life support to the four candidates who won on the day.

Jesse Jackson, having chalked up beforehand some remarkable

levels of support in overwhelmingly white states, had 'come home' to garner massive support from southern black voters. CBS exit polls showed that he received 90% or more of the votes of blacks in Alabama, Arkansas, Florida, Georgia, Louisiana, Maryland, Mississippi, North Carolina, Tennessee and Virginia. However, he also received well below 10% of white votes except in Virginia (12%) and Texas (9%).

Albert Gore had risked everything on Super Tuesday, hoping that southern white voters would catapult him into a leading position on the day and so generate a momentum to carry him to victory in subsequent primaries outside the South. He poured most of his $2 million war chest into these primaries and it paid dividends. He not only won more states than expected but came a very respectable second in four of the five states won by Jesse Jackson (and might have won some of them if the white vote had not been so divided).

Michael Dukakis's tally of five states included the two in New England held on Super Tuesday. But he also won in the two most populous states in the South – Florida and Texas – which he had deliberately targeted, as well as picking up Maryland. As a northerner he had run very respectably in a contest which could easily have polarized between the two standard-bearers of the white and black South – Gore and Jackson. He had ended the day narrowly behind Jackson and a nose ahead of Gore. Undoubtedly he benefited from commanding the best-financed organization in the race: he had 40 paid staff in Texas alone and spent twice as much as all his opponents combined in Florida.

For Richard Gephardt, apart from his expected victory in his home state of Missouri, there was not a great deal of comfort in the outcome. He came a poor second in Oklahoma and third in Florida. An early favourite to win Texas he had pulled out his organization to bolster what he thought was a faltering campaign in Iowa. In the event he was fatally squeezed between Dukakis and Gore. He still remained in the race but his early successes were now overshadowed by the rich pickings of his rivals.

The Democratic primary votes in the 16 Super Tuesday states divided as follows:

		%
Jackson	2,589,784	26.7
Dukakis	2,568,260	26.5
Gore	2,488,905	25.6
Gephardt	1,236,195	12.7
Others	823,492	8.5

So, no front-runner emerged as a result of the Democratic Super Tuesday strategy. If anything the result boosted the chances of

Jesse Jackson who certainly did not qualify as a presidential candidate electable in the South in the view of the southern Democratic establishment.

On the surface, the strategy of generating a momentum for voting Democrat in November appeared to have worked. Nearly 10 million voters participated in the Democratic contests on Super Tuesday, more than double the number who took part in the Republican contests. However, CBS exit polls showed that Republican primary voters were significantly more inclined to vote in November than Democrats. There was more cheerful news in the ABC exit polls which revealed that 37% of southern Democrats (a key element in both of Reagan's victories) could never vote for George Bush.

Having failed to win a single delegate in all the primaries and caucuses up to, and including, Super Tuesday, Gary Hart announced his withdrawal from the race on 11 March, in Colorado.

On 12 March, Jesse Jackson swept the Democratic caucuses in South Carolina with Albert Gore coming second, some way behind. This was not too surprising as this was one of the few states he won when he ran in the 1984 primaries. He was also born there and it is where his mother and grandmother still live.

Illinois was the next stop on the campaign trail for the remaining contenders. In the past it had played a critical role in setting the tone for subsequent primaries in northern industrial states. However, this time it was the home state of a candidate, Paul Simon, whom nobody thought could now win the nomination. But he won Illinois on 15 March. And in doing so he gave a major boost to Jesse Jackson (who came second) and delivered a blow to Michael Dukakis (who came a poor third). CBS exit polls showed that Jackson's success came from capturing 91% of the black vote (compared with 7% of the white vote). Although he performed well in some smaller industrial towns in the state, the bulk of his vote came from Chicago.

On 20 March, whereas the Republicans could only muster just under 4,000 voters in their primary in the territory of Puerto Rico, more than one-third of a million voters participated in the Democratic contest. Jesse Jackson won with 29% of the vote to Michael Dukakis's 23% and Paul Simon came third with 18%. On 22 March the Democrats Abroad announced the results of their own ballot in London, which went to Dukakis.

On 26 March more than 200,000 voters turned out to participate in the Democratic caucus in Michigan. Despite the support of Coleman Young, black Mayor of Detroit, Dukakis was soundly beaten into second place by Jackson. This was a further boost to the Jackson campaign outside the South. Despite their obvious disappointment, Dukakis supporters could point to the fact that Michigan was the only large state to hold a caucus rather than a primary and that only 3% of the voting-age population participated in the caucus.

On 28 March Richard Gephardt announced at a press conference on Capitol Hill, Washington that he too was abandoning the race. He declined to support any of the remaining candidates, saying that his delegates were free to do 'what they want when they get to the Convention'.

By now Dukakis needed a clear win in order to puncture the Jackson balloon and he secured it in Connecticut on 29 March. Although only 30,000 more people participated than in the Michigan caucus, it was a primary in a small state where the turnout was significantly higher. Dukakis won with 58% of the vote to Jackson's 28% in second place. It also restored Dukakis's lead in the national tally of convention delegates. As in Michigan he had carried suburbia and the small towns and rural areas, whilst Jackson had won the urban centres with their large minority populations. Dukakis admitted that he expected a long duel with Jackson, whose growing status throughout the race was indicated by a breakfast meeting he attended in Washington on 30 March. Instigated by former party chairman John White, the meeting provided Jackson with the opportunity to meet leading members of the Democratic establishment to discuss issues and policies. Mr White told reporters afterwards that the meeting showed Jackson was 'a mature candidate who recognizes that he has to get the trust and the confidence of the white party regulars'.

Whilst everyone had their eyes on the two megastate primaries of New York and Pennsylvania later in the month, there was the no small matter of Wisconsin to be dealt with first on 5 April. This was another Rust Belt state containing many of the key voting groups which would feature in the subsequent big primaries. As it turned out Jackson drew the crowds and Dukakis won the votes, securing a near 20% margin over Jackson in second place. CBS exit polls showed Dukakis winning 51% of the white vote and 9% of the black vote. It was no surprise, on past results, that Jackson won 88% of the black vote but he also achieved a remarkable 23% of the white vote. Albert Gore came third with 17% of the vote.

On 7 April, Paul Simon suspended his campaign whilst hanging on to his delegates. Meanwhile, attention turned remorselessly to New York which already promised to be the most bitter primary of the whole season. The candidate stirring the pot was Albert Gore. Following his success on Super Tuesday, where he was able to exploit his regional connections, he had been struggling to establish himself throughout the succeeding primaries in the rest of the country. New York was clearly his last throw and he chose to attack both Jackson and Dukakis before the poll. His main target was Jesse Jackson. He chose his ground as a staunch defender of Israel (with a little assistance from a $1 million advertising campaign) in order to win a large chunk of the Jewish vote. He expressed his dismay at Jackson's 'embrace of Arafat and Castro' and 'categorically rejected' Jackson's notion that 'there's a moral equivalence between Israel and the PLO'. Mayor Koch of New York City threw his own brickbats at Jackson, recalling his 1984 reference to New York City as 'Hymietown' and his public embrace of the controversial Islamic leader, Louis Farrakhan, who had called Judaism a 'gutter religion'. On the day Dukakis, the Spanish-speaking candidate with the Jewish wife who had stayed out of the catfight, won just over half the votes. Jesse Jackson came second with 37% and Albert Gore trailed in a poor third with 10%. CBS exit polls showed Dukakis had won 69% of the white and 38% of the Hispanic vote. Jackson had won 93% of the black and 61% of the Hispanic vote. The exit polls also revealed the collapse of Gore's strategy: he lost the Jewish vote to Dukakis by a margin of five-to-one (it seems that many of those frightened by Jackson threw their votes behind Dukakis as the man most likely to defeat him). Jackson's victories in the Delaware and Vermont caucuses were completely overshadowed by the New York primary.

New York did indeed mark the end of the race for Albert Gore. On 21 April the youngest candidate for either party suspended his campaign, admitting that he had failed to export his appeal beyond his native South. He declined to endorse any other candidate but said that the cause he had promoted would succeed, namely, 'to return the Democratic Party to its roots, to put the White House back on the side of working families and to once again stand up for a strong and intelligent American role in the world'.

New York also marked a turning point in the whole Democratic campaign. As the table at the end of this section shows, Jesse Jackson fought all the way to the end. But with the expected exception of the District of Columbia, Dukakis comfortably won every other subsequent state primary.

By the time he reached California (which he won with 61% of the votes) the scale of his achievement was clear. As late as December 1987, 74% of Americans polled did not know enough about him to have either a favourable or unfavourable view. Yet, in a poll by ABC after his poor performance in the Illinois primary in March, his approval rating amongst Democrats had risen to 62%. By May he had a commanding lead over Bush in the national polls which, with a dip in late June, he continued to hold through July (assisted by the coverage of the Democratic convention). Whilst Jackson had maintained an iron grip on the black vote throughout the primaries, Dukakis had won 46% of all the Hispanic votes cast (compared with

33% for Jackson). He had by far the largest campaign funds but he and his campaign had shown a coolness and professionalism under pressure which money alone could not buy.

Choosing a Running Mate

Michael Dukakis's search for a running mate began in earnest directly after he won the California primary on 7 June. Dukakis was leading Bush in polls in California and New Jersey, both of which last voted Democrat in 1964. They were even running level in heavily Republican Utah, which gave Reagan his biggest majorities in 1980 and 1984. But while Dukakis was encouraged by the poll data his campaign recognized that a great deal could change in five months and that the choice of running mate would be one of the crucial factors.

Most polls showed that he would beat George Bush but not with Jesse Jackson on the ticket. Jackson himself publically rejected the contention that he could cost the Democrats the election and said, 'We must have a progressive to balance the ticket.' He added that former Democratic Presidents Lyndon Johnson and Jimmy Carter both selected running mates, Hubert Humphrey and Walter Mondale respectively, with more progressive voting records than their own.

A number of American commentators saw Senator Sam Nunn of Georgia as an ideal choice. He is the chairman of the Senate Armed Services Committee and was considered by some the perfect balance on a ticket with Dukakis; a conservative southerner with the liberal north-easterner; an expert on defence with an expert on domestic policy, and a senator with a governor. But just a week after California Nunn told the *Boston Globe* that if offered the vice-presidential nomination 'I probably would not accept.'

Dukakis's campaign manager Paul Brountas was put in charge of the search for a running mate. He went down to Washington to discuss the question with leading Democrats in Congress. The Dukakis camp was urged to pick a southerner or westerner with foreign policy experience. He was also told that if Dukakis chose Jackson he could forget any chance of winning the election. On 18 June Senator Nunn announced that he had told Brountas that he did not want to be considered.

As well as Jackson and Nunn other candidates under consideration at this time included Senators Bill Bradley of New Jersey, John Glenn of Ohio, Bob Graham of Florida and Lloyd Bentsen of Texas, as well as Congressmen Thomas Foley of Washington and Lee Hamilton of Indiana. Neither Senator Al Gore nor Congressman Richard Gephardt featured prominently in the speculation of Washington commentators.

At the end of June an opinion survey conducted by the

Associated Press found that delegates to the Atlanta convention were quite happy to leave the choice up to Dukakis and did not want to force his hand. Nunn and Jackson got most support in the survey followed by Senators Glenn and Gore. Few mentioned Bentsen. At around the same time the list of possible choices narrowed. Nunn told Dukakis in person that he did not want the job, Bill Bradley said he didn't either and Thomas Foley indicated through an aide that he did not want to be considered.

On the 4 July holiday Dukakis invited Jackson to a family dinner at his home in Boston. After the dinner Jackson told reporters: 'My impression was that no decision has yet been made and that's why the meeting was so fruitful and alive ... the others under consideration are unknown quantities beyond their districts and beyond their home states.' Nevertheless the next day Dukakis held discussions with Al Gore and Richard Gephardt and on the following day met Lee Hamilton. Gephardt told the press that he would take the job if offered.

On 12 July Michael Dukakis ended the speculation and announced in Boston that Lloyd Bentsen would be his running mate. Dukakis clearly hoped his choice would revive memories of 1960, when Massachusetts' John F. Kennedy chose Texan Lyndon Johnson to join him on the ticket. They went on to beat an incumbent Republican vice-president. Bentsen, appearing with Dukakis in Boston said, 'The Massachusetts and the Texas axis was good for the country and good for the Democratic Party in 1960 and it's going to be a real winner in November 1988.' But nostalgia was not the main reason behind the selection. Dukakis hopes Bentsen will help him with key constituencies that do not naturally warm to the Massachusetts Governor. He is a southerner and more conservative than Dukakis. The choice was designed to reassure the white voters across the South who have abandoned the Democratic Party in recent elections. In particular Dukakis hopes it will improve his chances of taking Texas. The state accounts for 29 electoral college votes and no Democrat this century has won the White House without carrying the state. Bentsen won his Senate seat by beating George Bush in 1970 and the campaign hopes history will be repeated.

The choice of Bentsen angered many in Jesse Jackson's campaign. They felt their candidate had not been properly consulted. Benjamin Hooks, Director of the National Association for the Advancement of Colored People (NAACP), said black people might be inclined to withhold enthusiastic support from the Dukakis–Bentsen ticket. 'Sometimes we support enthusiastically, sometimes we just support, and sometimes we support with the brakes on,' he said. At a news conference Jackson could not hide his displeasure but he denied he was angry. 'I'm too controlled, I'm too clear, I'm too mature to be angry,' he said.

In the run up to Atlanta Michael Dukakis had the problem of convincing the electorate that he was not another big-spending liberal of the Humphrey–Mondale school who would happily raise taxes and would be soft on foreign policy. The choice of Bentsen was part of his strategy to allay moderates' fears but Dukakis recognized the need to do more than that. On the campaign trail he told voters: 'I've got a record. I've balanced nine budgets in a row. I've cut taxes five times in five years. I'm waging a real war, not a phoney war, against drugs. ... It will take tough, sustained and unrelenting enforcement ... at home and abroad, enforcement which uses the military where appropriate and necessary.' He called for a National Alliance Against Drugs, to be headed by the President, aimed at producing 'drug-free schools in every community in America in the 1990s'.

On defence Dukakis made clear his opposition to Star Wars but, addressing the Atlantic Council, set out plans for strengthening the European alliance. He gave this pro-NATO group his assessment of US–Soviet relations and called for negotiations between NATO and Warsaw Pact countries on conventional military forces.

The Dukakis campaign arranged a succession of 'photo opportunities' with police officers, emphasizing he would be tough on crime.

The Republicans, however, used every chance to point at Dukakis's supposedly liberal record. Bush criticized Dukakis for supporting a prison programme that allowed some convicted murderers in Massachusetts out on weekend release. President Reagan himself said Dukakis was a liberal. 'How other than liberal would you characterize a governor who in the last five years increased his state's spending twice as fast as the federal government's and more than a third faster than the average for all the other states?' the President asked.

The battlelines going into Atlanta were clear. Michael Dukakis knew that it was vital for him to succeed in convincing the public he was a moderate rather than an arch-liberal as the Republicans claimed.

The Atlanta Convention

Some 50,000 delegates, journalists and spectators descended on Atlanta during the weekend before the convention. The journalists represented 432 American newspapers, 165 magazines, 406 television stations, 274 radio stations and 260 photo services. In addition 400 foreign news organizations were there. The delegates numbered 4,160.

On the Sunday before the convention opened Jesse Jackson told more than 1,000 people at a Baptist church that floor fights over the vice-presidential nomination had happened before and were 'within the rules'. Meanwhile backroom talks between the Dukakis and Jackson campaign staffs continued. On the Monday morning of the convention Dukakis and Jackson held a three-hour meeting to try and heal the rift between them. They emerged apparently united. Dukakis said that although Jackson would not be the vice-presidential nominee he would be 'involved actively, fully, in a way that will bring us together and will bring the strongest grass-roots organization that has ever been built in a presidential campaign. Jesse Jackson won the votes of 7 million Americans and we need every single one of them.' Jackson said, 'We talked about building a coalition, we discussed matters of serious and substantive concern.'

Jackson publicly shook hands with Lloyd Bentsen. He declared that he would not challenge Bentsen for the vice-presidential nomination but would have his name put in nomination for the presidency. The serious split that the Dukakis people had feared had been avoided. The contest for the presidential nomination would be a symbolic gesture rather than a real challenge, and as such was acceptable to them.

In the convention centre itself, the opening session was dominated by speeches from former President Jimmy Carter and Ann Richards, the Texas State Treasurer. Carter joked, 'My name is Jimmy Carter, and I am not running for president,' in a reworking of his standard stump speech of 1976. In a short speech he appealed for party unity.

Ann Richards, who is expected to run for the governorship of Texas in 1990, was chosen to be the keynote speaker because of her biting wit. She told delegates George Bush couldn't help being born with a silver foot in his mouth and questioned his commitment to some of the issues he professes to care about. 'For eight straight years George Bush hasn't displayed the slightest interest in anything we care about. Now that he's after a job he can't get appointed to, he's like Columbus discovering America. He's found child care. He's found education.'

On Tuesday night Dukakis got his way on the party's platform, or election manifesto. The delegates adopted a 4,000-word document that committed the party to little that was either radical or unpopular. Delegates defeated by two-to-one Jackson's calls for higher taxes on the rich and a platform committing the United States and its allies to no first use of nuclear weapons. Another demand, for a pledge to support Palestinian self-determination, was debated but Jackson did not press a vote.

Later on Tuesday night Jackson brought the convention to its feet with an impassioned plea for unity. He told delegates,

'The only time we win is when we come together: if lions and lambs can find common ground, surely we can. He [Dukakis] has run a well-managed and a dignified campaign. No matter how tired or how tried, he always resisted the temptation to stoop to demagoguery. I have watched a good mind fast at work, with steel nerves, guiding his campaign out of the crowded field without appeal to the worst in us. His foreparents came to American in immigrant ships. My foreparents came to America on slave ships. But whatever the original ships, we are both in the same boat tonight.'

He set out his position as representative and champion of America's poor. 'I was born in the slum, but the slum was not born in me. And it wasn't born in you. You can make it.' Jackson explained that he would let his name go forward for the party's nomination as a symbol for the civil rights movement. He said it should be seen as 'a statement to the struggles of those who have gone before; as a legacy for those who will come after; as a tribute to the endurance, the patience, the courage of our forefathers and mothers; as an assurance that their prayers are being answered; their work was not in vain; and hope is eternal.'

On Wednesday night the convention did what everyone knew it would and nominated Michael Dukakis for the presidency. The final vote was 2,876 for Dukakis and 1,219 for Jackson. Mr Dukakis had been formally nominated by his fellow governor, Bill Clinton of Arkansas. He described the candidate as 'the kind of man who plays it straight, keeps his word, and pays his bills.' Reverend Jackson was nominated by the Machinists' Union President, William Winpisinger, who described his candidate in rather more stirring tones. He called Jackson 'a man of history, a mover, a shaker in the power struggles of freedom and tyranny, of democracy and autocracy.'

When the California delegation finally put Dukakis over the top, the band broke into the 'Washington Post March' and the convention centre erupted in excited cheering and sign-waving. The candidate watched the scene on television at his hotel. He allowed himself a smile. When the final votes had been counted, Jackson's campaign chairman, Willie Brown, proposed that 'in the spirit of the Jackson campaign and in the interests of unity' the nomination should be made unanimous. The motion was carried overwhelmingly. Now all that remained was the coronation.

Michael Dukakis came to the convention to deliver the traditional acceptance speech on Thursday night. Jesse Jackson was no small act to follow, especially for a man of such reserve. But to the delight of the delegates he delivered a powerful and, at times, emotional speech. He declared, 'If anyone tells you that the

American dream belongs to the privileged few and not to all of us, you tell them that the Reagan era is over ... and that a new era is about to begin.' He tackled the charge of 'liberalism' as well as setting out his stall for the election campaign when he said, 'This election is not about ideology. It's about competence.' He also struck at the Reagan administration's continuing scandals when he said the election was also 'about American values. Old-fashioned values like accountability and responsibility and respect for the truth.'

When the convention finished Dukakis and Bentsen set off on the campaign trail. ABC polling of delegates even before the convention showed that 93% felt that Dukakis could beat Bush in November (in 1984 only 53% of delegates thought Mondale could beat Reagan). Democratic activists felt for the first time in years that they were in with a chance of winning the White House.

| State | Democratic Primary Votes | | | |
	Dukakis	Jackson	Gore	Others
New Hampshire (16 Feb)	44,112	9,615	8,373	61,260
South Dakota (23 Feb)	22,367	3,866	5,990	39,438
Vermont (1 Mar)	28,353	13,044	–	9,394
Super Tuesday (8 Mar)				
Alabama	31,306	176,764	151,739	45,833
Arkansas	94,103	85,003	185,758	132,680
Florida	521,041	254,912	161,165	336,180
Georgia	97,179	247,831	201,490	76,252
Kentucky	59,433	49,667	145,988	63,633
Louisiana	95,667	221,532	174,974	132,277
Maryland	242,479	152,642	46,063	90,151
Mississippi	29,947	160,651	120,304	50,909
Missouri	61,303	106,386	14,549	345,567
North Carolina	137,993	224,177	235,669	82,119
Oklahoma	66,278	52,417	162,584	111,448
Tennessee	19,348	119,248	416,861	20,857
Texas	579,533	433,259	356,772	397,340
Virginia	80,183	164,709	81,419	38,588
Massachusetts	418,256	133,141	31,631	130,419
Rhode Island	34,211	7,445	1,939	5,434
Illinois (15 Mar)	245,289	484,233	77,265	694,141
Puerto Rico (20 Mar)	81,502	103,391	51,205	120,080
Connecticut (29 Mar)	140,291	68,372	18,501	14,231
Wisconsin (5 Apr)	483,172	285,995	176,712	68,903
New York (19 Apr)	801,457	585,076	157,559	31,094
Pennsylvania (26 Apr)	1,002,480	411,260	44,542	49,408
District of Columbia (3 May)	15,415	68,840	648	1,149
Indiana (3 May)	449,495	145,021	21,865	29,327
Ohio (3 May)	862,273	378,354	29,908	106,317
Nebraska (10 May)	106,334	43,380	2,519	16,775
West Virginia (10 May)	254,144	45,106	11,560	11,338
Oregon (17 May)	221,048	148,207	5,445	14,232
Idaho (24 May)	37,696	8,066	1,891	3,717
California (7 Jun)	1,800,609	1,050,576		118,729
Montana (7 Jun)	83,039	26,777		11,146
New Jersey (7 Jun)	406,634	209,873		26,072
New Mexico (7 Jun)	114,069	52,205		20,406

THE REPUBLICANS

The Republicans had gloated for months over the misfortunes of the Democratic candidates, so it was somewhat ironic that their delegate race opened in chaos and uproar. To begin with it started in the wrong place. The Republican caucus in Hawaii should have held its presidential preference vote on 27 January. However, this was rescheduled at the last minute for 4 February. The leading contenders at this stage included George Bush, Vice-President; Robert Dole, Senator for Kansas; General Alexander Haig, former Chief of Staff; Jack Kemp, Congressman for New York; Pierre du Pont, former Governor of Delaware; and the Revd Pat Robertson.

The Michigan convention, meeting over 29/30 January, was the first delegate contest, but the event was marred by bitter recriminations. George Bush had won the state primary in 1980, heavily defeating Ronald Reagan. This time Pat Robertson expected to win, his dedicated evangelical supporters having combined in previous months with those of Jack Kemp to win control of the party's state organization. But a combination of successful legal challenges by Bush supporters, and the eventual desertion of Kemp to Bush, finally defeated him. However, not before the nation had been treated to the remarkable spectacle of *two* conventions held in the same hotel – the 'Bush' convention upstairs and the 'Robertson' convention downstairs, both denouncing each other.

Pat Robertson had alleged that the Hawaii caucus date was deliberately put back in order to bury the result in the run up to Iowa. Whether or not he was correct, the effect was the same. Robertson scored an overwhelming 81.3% of support among the delegates to the state convention on 4 February and hardly anyone noticed.

To the great surprise of nobody at all Robert Dole swept the board in the county caucuses of his home state of Kansas held between 1 and 7 February.

The real upset of the Republican race came in Iowa on 8 February. Nearly 109,000 people attended the 2,487 Republican precinct caucuses and they delivered a massive rebuff to George Bush. The polls had already prepared him for the fact that Robert Dole would win (in a state where Bush had defeated Ronald Reagan in 1980). But he had little warning that he would finish a poor third behind Pat Robertson. The *Des Moines Register* (Iowa's biggest newspaper) published its own Iowa Poll, the last of which was virtually spot-on for all the candidates except Bush and Robertson. It gave Bush a 10% lead over Robertson but the final vote put Bush, at 18.6%, 6% behind Robertson. In the event Robertson's New Model Army of evangelical Christians, smarting from their unexpected reverse in Michigan, turned out in force.

Robert Dole had stood in Iowa in 1980 and received only 1.5% of the caucus votes, making victory this time all the sweeter. But sweetest of all was the humiliation of his main rival. Dole had been stung by the attacks upon him and his wife made by Bush campaign staff and had forced an angry confrontation with the Vice-President in the Senate a week before. The day after his defeat, George Bush said he still expected to win the Republican nomination: 'All it does is convince me to get the message out better.'

He succeeded in doing so in New Hampshire on 16 February, but not before seeming to stare defeat in the face. His tribulations were added to by Alexander Haig's formal announcement that he was retiring from the race on 12 February. He turned the event into a remarkable piece of political theatre, using it to endorse Robert Dole (who joined him in front of the cameras). As the media and the pollsters closed in on him, Bush fought back with a series of increasingly explicit anti-Dole television commercials, accusing him of not being able to 'say no' to taxes and favouring an oil import fee. He was undoubtedly assisted by Dole's tactical blunder in not responding to them.

The New Hampshire result halted the tide which had threatened to swamp Bush before the race had hardly begun. He achieved a 9% lead over Dole, to his evident relief. Dole claimed he had lost because of the Bush television campaign, and claimed a moral victory given that, before Iowa, he was trailing Bush by 20% in New Hampshire polls. But he shocked many people in a television interview on the very night of the result: asked if he had any message for his rival, George Bush, he snarled, 'Yes, stop telling lies about me.' In those few seconds he brought to the surface all the old charges of his 'mean' streak and his reputation in the 1976 campaign as a hatchet man. Pat Robertson had said that he would come third or possibly second: but he finished fifth and last. On 18 February, Pete du Pont announced that he was withdrawing from the race through lack of funds and did not endorse any of the remaining candidates. But the biggest casualties in New Hampshire were the polls: post-Iowa they had shown Dole rapidly closing the gap on Bush (a late Gallup poll gave Dole an 8% lead) and they had overwhelmingly suggested a close contest.

The swings and roundabouts of US politics took another turn only a week later. The main focus of attention turned towards the South, which was to make up the bulk of the states polling on Super Tuesday in March, but before that there was a caucus in Minnesota and a primary in South Dakota on 23 February. Dole won both decisively, securing 42.6% of the votes in the Minnesota caucus and 55% of the primary vote in South Dakota. Pat Robertson came second and George Bush third in both states.

Bush stopped campaigning in South Dakota and put only a minimal effort into Minnesota in order to concentrate upon the Super Tuesday states, but Dole naturally made the most of his rival's defeat.

Throughout February there was a clutch of small caucuses: Bush won in Nevada but with barely one-quarter of the votes and he also carried Maine; Dole won Wyoming and Pat Robertson won Alaska. However, in the first week of March, George Bush turned the tables again and carried the Vermont primary (1 March) with 49% of the votes cast, 10% ahead of Dole. Much more significant was the primary in South Carolina (5 March), the only one of the former Confederate states in the South not to poll on 'Super Tuesday'. It was seen as a foretaste of how the rest of the South would vote three days later. If this assessment was correct then George Bush had grounds for rejoicing because he won the state with 48% of the votes, leaving Dole the sole (and rather dubious) consolation of coming second, only 1.5% ahead of Pat Robertson. With more than a passing thought for conservative voters on 'Super Tuesday' George Bush had held a meeting before polling day in South Carolina where he shared the platform with former Senator Barry Goldwater, the doyen of the Right. Bush praised him as one who had 'come to see his ideas prevail and his agenda triumph'.

Super Tuesday: The candidates had flocked to the South as soon as the New Hampshire vote was declared. The intervening contests were duly analyzed but everyone was waiting for the bumper harvest on 8 March. George Bush was the clear favourite in the polls (in marked contrast to his poor performance in the South when he fought Ronald Reagan for the 1980 nomination). His well-funded, well-oiled campaign had been working flat out in the area for many months. He must also have sighed with relief when returning to campaign in his adopted state of Texas and throughout a region where President Reagan's personal stock stood so high (which his vice-president hoped to capitalize upon). However, for all the polls, Super Tuesday represented uncharted waters, with campaigning effort and organization stretched across so many states at the same time.

In the event, George Bush delivered a killer punch to his opponents, sweeping up all 14 southern and border states, plus the two in New England. His vote share fell below 50% in only four. The Bush juggernaut crushed Dole everywhere except Missouri, North Carolina (the birthplace of Elizabeth Dole) and Oklahoma. Robertson came second in only two states, whilst Kemp's highest vote was 7% in Massachusetts. The table overleaf sets out the total votes for each candidate in the 16 state primaries:

		%
Bush	2,761,045	56.9
Dole	1,151,887	23.7
Robertson	624,814	12.9
Kemp	235,259	4.9
Others	80,379	1.7

Exit poll data revealed that Bush's greatest support tended to come from older voters and, in certain states (particularly Arkansas, North Carolina, Tennessee and Texas), more from men than women. Bush had been careful to gear his campaign to the conservative mood of the South and put his message across by pouring huge amounts of money into television commercials. The result was that, in one day, he had scooped up 574 delegates and created a momentum which, on all previous experience, would now be unstoppable. Whilst almost twice as many people voted in the Democratic primaries on Super Tuesday, he was encouraged by the evidence of CBS exit polls which showed that Republican primary voters were significantly more likely than Democrats to take part in the November presidential election.

For Robert Dole, 8 March was an unmitigated disaster. He viewed the results from Chicago, where he had gone to prepare for the next, Illinois primary. As the scale of his defeat unfolded on the television screen Richard Nixon sent him a telegram urging him to fight on. He was determined to do precisely that but he could not fail to reflect upon his increasingly desperate position. His campaign had been poorly organized because he did not delegate. Following his New Hampshire defeat there had been the highly public sacking of two senior staff members. His campaign had also wasted money at an alarming rate (staff had exceeded their budget by 50% before the election year had even begun and ended up having to slash their planned expenditure on television advertising for 'Super Tuesday' by more than two-thirds).

The results were just as disastrous for Pat Robertson. He had banked heavily upon making a significant impact in the southern 'Bible Belt' which was his own home territory but he was crushed even more comprehensively than Dole. Indeed, whilst ABC's exit polls on Super Tuesday found 39% of Republican primary voters describing themselves as Born-Again Christians, Bush captured more of their votes than Robertson in all states except Oklahoma. Just prior to the South Carolina primary, former Republican congressman Peter McCloskey stated that Robertson's father (a US senator) had pulled strings to keep his son out of the combat area in the Korean war. Robertson began a $35 million lawsuit but then, on 2 March, he abandoned it. These damaging allegations were not the principal cause of his failure but, added to his blunders about Soviet missiles in Cuba and claims to have insider information on the whereabouts of US hostages in Lebanon, they did not help. He had been determined to win in South Carolina but came third. On Super Tuesday he came second in only Texas and Louisiana and secured only seven delegates out of all the primaries held that day.

On 10 March, conservative New York congressman Jack Kemp withdrew from the race. For much of the Reagan years he had been a leading representative of the Right, promoting the case for supply-side economics. His bid to capture the conservative wing of the Republican Party had, in the end, been thwarted by the competition from fellow conservatives, Pat Robertson and Pete du Pont.

Those remaining in the race moved their campaigns to Illinois where Dole desperately needed to slow the momentum of Bush's Super Tuesday victory. However, the polls showed that the Vice-President was on track to win the state primary comfortably. As if in recognition of this, on 10 March Dole abruptly cancelled all his television advertising and announced that he was sacking half of his campaign staff across the country. His aides were privately urging him to quit before the Illinois vote in order to avoid another humiliating defeat, but Dole declared that he was not pulling out. He was also under increasing pressure from within the Republican Party to withdraw in order to allow George Bush a clear run which, it was hoped, would contrast greatly with the still-divided Democrats. His answer was the polls, which consistently showed that he would be the tougher man of the two for the Democrats to beat in November. Meanwhile, George Bush revelled in his recent victories and the support of the state's Republican establishment. He refused Dole's challenge to a half-hour televised debate as state-wide polls showed him heading for an overwhelming victory. And so it turned out. On 15 April he won 54.7% of the primary votes (compared to the 48% Reagan vote in the 1980 primary here), to Bob Dole's 36% and Pat Robertson's 7%. Dole indicated that he would stay in the race at least until the Wisconsin primary on 5 April.

On 20 March, just under 4,000 people took part in the Republican primary in Puerto Rico and 97% voted for George Bush. But attention was focused upon Connecticut in the reasonable expectation of a somewhat larger turnout. On 29 March primary voters in Connecticut gave an overwhelming endorsement to George Bush (70.6% of the total votes cast). On the evening of polling day Robert Dole formally withdrew from the race. He sought to assist party unity by vowing to support the candidature of George Bush: 'The bottom line is keeping the White House Republican.'

The race was now left between Bush and Robertson. But as everyone knew, it was a race only in name. Electorally, Pat Robertson was by now a 'busted flush' and George Bush, barring any catastrophe, was set to coast his way to the New Orleans convention in August. However, this in itself presented a major problem. Precisely because there was now no longer any real contest in the Republican race, media attention inevitably turned to the Democrats. George Bush was left to pick up a whole series of state primaries which had yet to poll but which were of diminishing interest to anyone except political insiders.

However, interest had not waned in the activities of the administration of which he was Vice-President. On the same day as the Connecticut primary a number of senior staff in the Justice Department resigned over the conduct of the special prosecutor's investigation into Attorney-General Edwin Meese's role in an aborted $1 billion Iraqi pipeline deal. Two days later, the joint congressional committees on the Iran–Contra scandal released a piece of paper containing handwritten notes of the former National Security Advisor, Rear-Admiral John Poindexter. The 27-word note, dated 17 January 1986, concerned the proposed arms sales to Iran and registered George Bush's presence at the meeting where this matter was discussed, casting further doubt on his public denial of knowledge of the whole arms sale operation.

Waiting in the Wings
As the table of results at the end of this section shows, Bush romped through the remaining Republican primaries. But he emerged at the end of the process with an uphill battle to win the presidency itself. He was behind in the polls and his position as heir to the Reagan legacy was a less attractive prize than would have seemed possible a couple of years ago. A Media General–Associated Press poll in early June showed that a majority of Americans would not support the President for a third term even if the Constitution allowed it. In 1984, Reagan won the support of 25% of Democrats and 63% of independent voters. But in the survey, just 13% of Democrats and 27% of independents said they would vote for him for a third term.

Republican strategists, however, argued that the Dukakis lead over Bush was a temporary phenonemon reflecting the appeal of a new face who had not yet been subjected to close scrutiny. Bush's chief of staff, Lee Atwater was, publicly at least, confident about his man's chances. He said, 'No matter what the polls look like this is going to be a close election because the Vice-President has an advantage in the Electoral College.' He thought there were between 210 and 220 electoral college votes 'easily available'. He saw the problem as gathering the other 60 or so needed to win.

The speculation about who would be the Republican vice-presidential candidate was less intense than on the Democratic side. A late July *USA Today* poll among Republican delegates who were to attend the party convention in New Orleans showed 21% preferring Bob Dole as the running mate whilst 16% favoured Jack Kemp (others who also featured were Elizabeth Dole and ex-White House Chief of Staff, Howard Baker). The candidate said he would not seriously consider his choice until after the Democrats' convention. The Washington press did not believe that but nevertheless most of their attention went on the more dramatic story of Dukakis's vice-presidential selection and his rejection of Jackson.

In June and July Bush set out on a broad electoral strategy aimed at widening his electoral base. He told anti-Castro Cubans, 'There have been no accommodations made with Castro's corrupt communist government by this administration and, if I may inject a partisan point, I guarantee you there will be no accommodations.' He pleased the Hispanics by promising to appoint at least one Hispanic to the cabinet if elected. He appealed to liberals by choosing New Jersey Governor Thomas Kean as the keynote speaker for the Republican convention in New Orleans. Aware that he trailed Dukakis amongst women voters he made moves to close the so-called 'gender gap'. He appointed a woman, Sheila Tate, as his chief press adviser and pointed to gains women had achieved during the Reagan years: 'More than half of the new jobs have gone to women, and the unemployment rate for women is now as low as it is for men – a milestone in our economic history,' he said. He addressed the National Association for the Advancement of Colored People and said he would do better than expected amongst black voters. Many present thought he was trying to distance himself from the Reagan administration's record on civil rights enforcement.

But despite Bush's attempts to make his electoral base as wide as possible he still faced the problems associated with being part of the administration. The Vice-President worked hard to dissociate himself from what had become known as the 'sleaze factor'. A massive fraud investigation in the Pentagon prompted Bush to call a press conference. He told journalists that if elected he would not 'tolerate lawlessness in the Pentagon, in the streets or in the Congress'. He added, 'I won't mince words, I am offended and shocked at the abuse that these allegations represent.'

The Bush campaign continued to be hurt by the allegations of impropriety levelled against Attorney-General Edwin Meese. He did not criticize him openly but when Meese resigned the Vice-President issued a statement saying, 'Ed did the right thing and I wish him well.' Nevertheless the Dukakis campaign made capital of the events surrounding Meese's departure. Michael Dukakis declared, 'This administration's inability to set high standards for public service will not be solved by the Meese resignation. This administration has had one scandal after another, one resignation after another.'

But Bush also made good use of the advantages of incumbency. Following the shooting down of an Iranian airbus by an American warship on 3 July, he personally put the American case at the Security Council of the United Nations. There was no precedent for the appearance of an American vice-president at the head of the UN delegation but the appearance helped create the impression that he was experienced in foreign policy and that, unlike his opponent, he was already part of the national decision-making process.

Following the successful Democratic convention Bush's ratings slipped again against Dukakis. President Reagan launched into the fray, accusing the Democrats of trying to deceive the voters. Using one of his radio broadcasts he declared: 'You'll never hear that 'L' word – liberal – from them. ... They've put on political trenchcoats and dark glasses and slipped their platform into a brown wrapper.' The gloves were off and it looked as if America was in for a rough, ill-tempered ride to November.

A graphic illustration of how rough things might become came in the rumours about the mental health of Michael Dukakis. Supporters of right-wing extremist Lyndon LaRouche were believed to have spread the stories at the Democratic convention, claiming that Dukakis had twice been treated for depression: once, after his brother Stelian was killed in a 1973 road accident; and again after he was defeated in his 1978 bid for re-election as Governor of Massachusetts. The rumours were strongly denied by Dukakis's doctor. However, President Reagan fanned the flames when he was asked to comment on the rumours at a White House press conference on 3 August. He replied: 'Look, I'm not going to pick on an invalid.' Following the uproar from the press corps, he was obliged to convene another conference, half an hour later, at which he said he had been joking and 'I don't think I should have said what I said.' The plot thickened when senior staff at CBS television, the *Wall Street Journal* and *Los Angeles Times* claimed that Bush aides had been peddling the rumours, charges strenuously denied by the Bush camp.

Overshadowed by these events was the resignation of James Baker as US Treasury Secretary to take charge of the Bush election campaign. Twelve years earlier he had performed the same function for Gerald Ford and, although unsuccessful, had still managed to bring his candidate from 30% behind in the polls to narrow defeat. He would have been greatly encouraged by the decision of President Reagan to devote a great deal of time to the Bush campaign – offering to appear at least twice a week in support of the ticket between Labor Day and the election itself.

The New Orleans Convention

At first sight New Orleans lacked the drama of Atlanta. The Democratic convention had all the human interest surrounding Jesse Jackson and the way he and his supporters would react to the Dukakis nomination. The Republican convention never expected to match that (even if it wanted to) but it did have the advantage of the President's farewell. As George Bush remained in Washington, Ronald Reagan took the spotlight with his speech delivered on Monday night. It was a nostalgic swan-song, reviewing what had been achieved in his eight years of office; but it also aimed at boosting George Bush's chances of keeping the White House safe in Republican hands: 'I care that we give custody of this office to someone who will build on our changes, not retreat to the past.... So, George, I'm in your corner.' Passing the leadership of the Republican Party to George Bush, he told the ecstatic delegates, 'I'll leave my 'phone number and address behind just in case you need a foot soldier.'

President Reagan met George Bush briefly the next morning at Belle Chasse naval air station near New Orleans as he flew out to California, leaving the centre stage clear for the candidate. Bush himself was under increasing pressure to name his vice-presidential running mate. On Monday he said he had narrowed the list of candidates but had not picked one. He would only comment that 'I think my choice will be widely accepted.' That same day, Elizabeth Dole said she did not expect to be named and her husband, Robert Dole, said he had done nothing to try to influence Bush: 'It's his call.'

On Tuesday, the convention approved the Republican platform for the election. Entitled 'An American Vision: For Our Children and Our Future', it ran to 104 pages and was eight times longer than the Democratic platform approved in Atlanta. In addition to a commitment to make NATO allies 'bear their fair share of the defense burden' it followed the conservative line by pledging no tax increases, support for SDI and a constitutional amendment to ban abortion. However, it also reflected the priorities of the candidate (concerned at months of Democratic campaigning as the 'party of the family') by including proposals for child-care tax credits for low-income families, a new programme of 'merit schools', and tax-free savings bonds to help pay for the expense of college education. Doubtless goaded by Democratic criticism it also promised stronger action against those engaged in the drugs trade. It was made clear that these proposals were consistent with George

Bush's pledge to freeze overall government spending. There was no debate or dissent when the platform was presented and approved by a half-empty convention hall.

Tuesday also brought unwelcome news in the form of worsening US trade figures. Before seasonal adjustments the trade deficit rose from $9.5 billion in May to $12.6 billion in June as high consumer demand continued, with attendant fears of future inflation.

The real surprise of the convention came with Bush's announcement of his vice-presidential nominee on Tuesday night. Skipping a formidable generation of Republican warriors, he selected the 41-year-old Senator Dan Quayle, from Indiana. The choice certainly surprised many attending the convention but was welcomed by the conservative wing of the party. It was hoped that his youthfulness and good looks would appeal to the post-war generation of voters and help redress the large Democratic lead among women voters.

At his first press conference, with George Bush at his side, he gained an early taste of the pressures to come as he had to field questions about his relative inexperience; his 1980 golfing weekend with a female lobbyist who later appeared in *Playboy* magazine; and, more importantly, questions which contrasted his strong views about defence with his joining the National Guard rather than serving in Vietnam. This last issue clouded what should have been a triumphant climax to the convention for George Bush. Quayle was pulled out of several planned television interviews as Bush aides buried themselves in urgent meetings where they discussed what could be done to limit the damage of these allegations.

In his speech on Wednesday night Bush sought to put the issue to one side when he declared 'I'm proud to have Dan Quayle at my side.' The speech was undoubtedly a personal triumph for Bush as he stepped firmly out of Ronald Reagan's shadow. He told the cheering delegates: 'I mean to run hard, to fight hard, to stand on the issues – and I mean to win.' Turning to the large poll leads which his rival Michael Dukakis had held for most of the year he said, 'There are a lot of great stories in politics about the underdog winning and this is going to be one of them.' But his main purpose was to inspire his party troops with a vision of things to come. He pledged himself to create 30 million jobs in the next eight years (doubling the record of the Reagan administrations). He told the delegates 'We are on the verge of a new century ... I say it will be another American century. Our work is not done. Our force is not spent.'

But, as the debris was being cleared away from the New Orleans convention hall, George Bush might have reflected that now he was on his own. Whether or not he defeated the 'Curse of Van Buren' (the last serving vice-president to be elected president, 152 years ago) was solely in his hands. Others may have reflected, as Macaulay did of John Dryden, 'That he may soar, it is only necessary that he should not struggle to fall.' His choice of Dan Quayle had been a personal one and it had marred an otherwise impeccably stage-managed convention. Nobody questioned his determination to fight and win, but doubts were inevitably raised about his judgment and fears expressed about whether any more 'gaffes' would be forthcoming.

| State | Republican Primary Votes | | | |
	Bush	Dole	Robertson	Others
New Hampshire (16 Feb)	59,290	44,797	14,775	38,763
South Dakota (23 Feb)	17,404	51,599	18,310	6,092
Vermont (1 Mar)	23,565	18,655	2,452	3,160
South Carolina (5 Mar)	94,738	40,265	37,261	23,028
Super Tuesday (8 Mar)				
Alabama	137,807	34,733	29,776	11,199
Arkansas	32,114	17,667	12,918	5,606
Florida	559,820	191,197	95,826	54,379
Georgia	215,516	94,749	65,163	25,500
Kentucky	72,020	27,868	13,526	7,988
Louisiana	83,687	25,626	26,295	9,173
Maryland	107,026	64,987	12,860	15,881
Mississippi	104,814	26,855	21,378	5,825
Missouri	168,812	164,394	44,705	22,389
North Carolina	124,260	107,032	26,861	15,648
Oklahoma	78,224	73,016	44,067	13,631
Tennessee	152,515	55,027	32,015	14,695
Texas	648,178	140,795	155,449	70,534
Virginia	124,738	60,921	32,173	16,310
Massachusetts	141,113	63,392	10,891	25,785
Rhode Island	10,401	3,628	911	1,095
Illinois (15 Mar)	469,151	309,253	58,722	21,130
Puerto Rico (20 Mar)	3,857	109	5	2
Connecticut (29 Mar)	73,501	21,005	3,191	6,474
Wisconsin (5 Apr)	295,295	28,460	24,798	10,741
New York (19 Apr)	No preference vote: delegate selection only			
Pennsylvania (26 Apr)	687,323	103,763	79,463	–
District of Columbia (3 May)	5,890	469	268	93
Indiana (3 May)	351,829	42,878	28,712	14,236
Ohio (3 May)	643,907	94,650	56,347	–
Nebraska (10 May)	138,784	45,572	10,334	9,359
West Virginia (10 May)	109,284	–	10,539	–
Oregon (17 May)	199,938	49,128	21,212	4,173
Idaho (24 May)	55,464	–	5,876	6,935
California (7 Jun)	1,805,070			375,139
Montana (7 Jun)	62,863			23,044
New Jersey (7 Jun)	236,140			14,302
New Mexico (7 Jun)	68,454			19,691
North Dakota (14 Jun)	36,572			2,388

CHAPTER FIVE

The Candidates

THE DEMOCRATS

Michael Stanley Dukakis

BORN:	3 November 1933, Boston, Massachusetts.
PARENTS:	Father: Panos Dukakis, physician. Mother: Euterpe (Bourkis).
MARRIED:	Katharine 'Kitty' Dickson (once divorced), 1963. Three children: John, 30 (stepson – adopted); Andrea, 23; and Kara, 20.
EDUCATION:	Graduated in Political Science from Swarthmore College, 1955. Phi Beta Kappa. Gained law degree at Harvard Law School, cum laude, 1960.
MILITARY SERVICE:	US Army, 1955–7. Left as a Private.
CAREER: 1960–74	Hill & Barlow, Boston, attorney.
1963–71	Massachusetts State Representative, serving four terms.
1966	Ran unsuccessfully for State Attorney-General.
1970	Ran unsuccessfully for Lieutenant-Governor of Massachusetts.
1971–73	Presented weekly TV current affairs programme, 'The Advocates'.
1975–79	Governor of Massachusetts – lost 1978 bid for re-election.
1979–82	Harvard University; Lecturer, Director of Intergovernmental Studies, John F. Kennedy School of Government.
1983–85	Governor of Massachusetts (second term).
1986–	Governor of Massachusetts (third term).

There is something of the plodding mule about Michael Dukakis. Perhaps this personification of the party's symbol made him shine out amongst the 'Seven Dwarfs' (as the press dubbed the Democratic hopefuls) when they lined up at the start of the primary circuit. His campaign plodded along, relentless and unswerving – some would say dull – and it is difficult to pinpoint exactly what made 5-ft 8-in Dukakis stand out from the rest of the Democratic field.

He is relatively youthful in presidential terms – his 55th birthday is five days before the election – and until his candidacy was announced he was little more than an unrecognizable name. His wife, Kitty, quipped that people thought 'Dukakis' was the bottom line of an eye-chart. In last year's American 'Who's Who', George Bush's wife, Barbara, commanded an entry of thirteen lines. Michael Dukakis was summed up in less than six, in spite of being named by *Newsweek* as the nation's most effective governor.

It has been suggested that the American public are more interested in the personality than the party of their presidential candidates. Bush is not going to score many points in this game but neither is Dukakis. He has been described as having the 'poetry of a slide rule' (because he lacks passion in his speeches); as a political 'word processor' (for his verbosity); as a 'calculator on legs' (for his technocratic style of government); as 'an ernest nerd' (by one of his own aides); as 'Zorba the Clerk' (by those who find him boring); as 'the shrimp' (by those who find his stature diminutive); and as 'the Duke' (by those who find his character statuesque). Someone when asked what make he would be, if he were a type of car, said, 'A Honda Civic – compact, efficient, reliable, short on style and long on utility.' He says he would rather be an all-American Chevrolet.

These days the American public's perception of their candidates depends largely on media coverage and Dukakis should be adept at making the most of media opportunities. He has been a newspaper columnist, once ran a radio show and hosted a current affairs series on television. So what does the media machine make of Michael Stanley Dukakis?

Any presidential hopeful must play up his image as a 'self-made' man: it is, after all, a vital ingredient in the American Dream. Dukakis qualifies by virtue of his ethnic origins. True, his parents did come to America from Greece, but the young Michael was hardly raised in a ghetto. His father, Panos, was the first Greek immigrant to graduate from Harvard Medical School and his mother, Euterpe, distinguished herself at college and worked as a teacher before they started their family. The Dukakis parents were 'immigrant superachievers': they started from a point of cultural (and linguistic) disadvantage but gained ground rapidly, setting high standards for their sons, Stelian and Michael. By the time the latter was born, the family lived in the comfortable Boston suburb of Brookline (also the birthplace of John F. Kennedy, as Dukakis's campaign literature takes pains to remind us). Michael was actually raised in a secure middle-class environment – a fact which should do him little harm in the polling stakes since the vast majority of voters perceive themselves as 'middle class'. By the time of his death in 1979, Panos Dukakis had accumulated a multi-million-dollar legacy which he placed in trust for his family.

The overzealous emphasis on Dukakis's origins during the campaign has been parodied. *Time* magazine called him an 'everyethnic'; Greek by descent: Jewish by marriage; and Hispanic by virtue of his fluency in Spanish. No doubt the 'ethnic' tag has brought him a few votes in the primaries (and, perhaps, even lost him a few in the more conservative WASP-ish areas).

His mother recalls that his first words were 'monos mou' – 'by myself' in Greek. It is not important whether Euterpe's reminiscence is accurate; the phrase is appropriate for the Dukakis image of independence, determination and self-discipline. Contemporaries say he was a responsible, unrebellious child. A successful scholar through sheer hard work rather than natural aptitude, he opted not to go straight to Harvard as he might have done. Instead he attended the smaller but academically renowned college of Swarthmore, near Philadelphia. It seems he was a conscientious student and worked steadily, never 'cramming' for exams. He still claims, with pride, that he has never stayed up all night for anything.

The controlled Dukakis student regime did leave time for taking part in college sports and college politics. Not that the latter were in any way disruptive. Dukakis was part of the 'silent generation', the post-war, pre-1960s idealists. The memories of Hitler's impassioned speeches and political fervour were still fresh in their minds and Dukakis shunned political passion for what he saw to be more effective means of action: crusades for reform, active debate and votes for consensus. When the revolutionary 1960s arrived Dukakis did not take part in protest marches for fashionable causes. He agreed with the protesters' ideals but not with their methods. This political composure and disdain for what he sees as wasted energy has remained with Dukakis and is probably responsible for what his critics identify as a lack of passion in his addresses and an inability to motivate his audience.

After graduation he performed his military service with competence but without any apparent enthusiasm. He served in Korea, entering the army as a private and departing two years later without progression. It must have been a time of complete tedium for the successful Dukakis. He seemed to regard it as a necessary but unrewarding task which, once completed, freed him to study at Harvard Law School.

In 1960 he joined Hill and Barlow, a law practice in Boston, and set about moving into local political life. He and like-minded friends campaigned on a 'reform' ticket. Being a high-minded Brookliner, Dukakis was highly critical of the backstabbings, personal loyalties and casual corruption which seemed an integral part of the rest of Massachusetts political life. He also found the cliques and ruling powers elitist and unfavourable to someone of his background. Determining to restore integrity and public service to the state, he campaigned on a 'Good Government' ticket; he and his team became known as 'Goo-Goos'.

He ran successfully for the Massachusetts state legislature in 1962 and served four terms as state representative. But he fell foul of the Democratic Party establishment and only found support among the 'young blood' of the state. He ran unsuccessfully both for attorney-general of the state in 1966 and for lieutenant-governor in 1970, so in 1974 he turned all his efforts to campaigning for the gubernatorial elections.

The state of Massachusetts was in bad shape. Unemployment was up and a large but undisclosed deficit was rumoured. Dukakis ran an aggressive and arrogant campaign, promising to solve the problems without raising taxes as his opponent would. He maintained that the key lay in better management of the state's finances. However, after a remarkable landslide victory, the new Governor discovered the situation was far worse than he had anticipated. The $300-million deficit rose daily. Dukakis stubbornly refused to renege on his campaign promises. He slashed welfare benefits but the debts kept mounting. When they finally reached $600 million he had no option but to raise taxes.

He had lost his policy battle on all fronts and he was also making mistakes in other areas of his administration. Being over-keen to oust all traces of the old establishment's ways, he refused not only to grant favours to the team who had helped elect him but categorically refused to become involved when they applied for new positions in the administration. His friends felt abandoned. His popularity rapidly declined.

By the time he ran for re-election in 1978, the financial situation in the state was beginning to improve but Dukakis's popularity was not. He suffered a humiliating defeat which has since become a legendary part of the Dukakis history. Kitty said it was like 'public death' for him. His son John said he found him sitting, silently contemplating his mistakes for hours on end. His opponents assert that this is one of the occasions when he sought psychiatric help for depression. Dukakis says that he simply went off to think things over and took a teaching position at Harvard's John F. Kennedy

School of Government. Being a pragmatist, Dukakis has since managed to use even this, the blackest spot on his record sheet, to advantage in his personal mythology. He almost cites it as his necessary humiliation – the humanizing flaw in what would otherwise have been a slightly too perfect career.

By 1982 a 'new' Dukakis was on the election trail with a campaign managed by John Sasso. He had learnt important lessons, he maintained. He had learnt to listen and he had a new formula for reducing the state deficit. He would instigate a clamp-down on unpaid taxes to raise revenue and start an employment and training programme to get recipients off welfare. It worked: the 'new' Dukakis was elected and his plans were successful.

From 1983 onwards the financial fortunes of Massachusetts did a complete about-face. They called it the 'Massachusetts Miracle', and the Massachusetts Governor was naturally keen to take the credit for it. Sceptics point out that the national situation was improving and expansion of high-technology industries (many, ironically, working on defence projects approved by the Reagan administration) into the state brought a healthier balance sheet. Dukakis's tax and work programmes undoubtedly had their merits; how much they actually contributed to the miracle is difficult to quantify. But Governor Dukakis was re-elected in 1986 with another landslide victory.

After the disastrous 1984 Mondale–Ferraro campaign, John Sasso suggested that Dukakis would be an ideal presidential candidate and whilst Dukakis dragged his feet initially, he soon grew enthusiastic about the idea. He decided the main theme of his campaign would be to repeat the Massachusetts miracle nation-wide along with a drive for 'good jobs at good wages'. At a time of record national deficit, it has proved tempting bait.

The campaign has not been without its mishaps. John Sasso had to resign in disgrace after it was proved that he had orchestrated a smear campaign, without Dukakis's knowledge, against the plagiarizing Senator Joe Biden. Dukakis was shattered to lose an old friend from his team but the tough and determined campaign manager Susan Estrich took over and there seems to have been little flak from the incident since.

Probably still stung by earlier mistakes, Dukakis has meticu-lously avoided concrete promises *en route* to his nomination at the 1988 Atlanta convention. He has declared that he wants to limit the power of Political Action Committees (PACs) (from whom he accepts no funds himself) and he wants to begin a programme of Regional Economic Development Conferences. But little else. He is known to oppose aid to the Contras. He wants to strengthen the authority of the United Nations and continue an arms-control dialogue with the USSR. He is against SDI, MX missiles, Trident and B1 bombers and he is in favour of strengthening conventional forces.

If he has an Achilles' heel, it is probably his experience – or rather, inexperience – especially in foreign affairs. The only foreign expeditions mentioned during his campaign have been a study vacation in Peru, his national service in Korea, and a 1976 trip to Pelopi on the Greek island of Lesbos, site of his fathers' ex-familial home. George Bush's official profile boasts visits to over 70 countries. In the past this lack of experience might have been a serious handicap to Dukakis but it is less likely to be so in this election. With the success of recent arms reduction talks and a generally more peaceful climate around the world, the American public, traditionally introspective, looks set to become even less interested in global affairs in the near future. To cope with any heckling on foreign policy issues, Dukakis has the expert advice of Georgetown Professor Madeleine Albright on his campaign team. This seems to have served him well so far but it would not be surprising if Bush mounted an assault on this weakness in the televised pre-election debates. These debates are the traditional gladiatorial arena. The goal is to take a swipe at each other's images. The prizes are measured in poll points.

Neither of this year's presidential candidates offers great promise in terms of charisma. Dukakis tries to sound interesting. He says he loves to read but his wife says she has never known him pick up a novel. Even books must be functional for the pragmatic Governor. No frills, no elaborations: 'What you see is what you get', as Mama Dukakis has said of him. But certain idiosyncrasies suggest that the Governor may not be quite the two-dimensional character his mother would have us believe. Take his 25-year marriage to Kitty.

Katharine Dickson hardly constituted the ideal partner for serious young Attorney Dukakis when they first started dating. At 24, Kitty had a failed marriage behind her and a 3-year-old son. She came from a Jewish show-business family and was an accomplished dancer. Initially his parents were shocked that Michael was taking on a divorcee with a young child. But he had made up his mind and was characteristically immovable. The couple were married in 1963 and appear to have been very happy ever since, in spite of the many differences between them.

Kitty is highly-strung and impulsive; Michael sometimes pauses so long for thought, he can unnerve even a seasoned interviewer. Kitty has taken up a campaign against drug abuse since declaring last year that she had previously broken a 26-year addiction to amphetamine diet pills. No one seems to recall health-conscious Michael even drinking to excess and his critics' allegations of a history of depression forced the revelation of a medical record showing nothing more serious than a tonsillectomy.

Then there is the question of money. Kitty is, by her own admission, extravagant. Michael makes a campaign issue of the 'good housekeeping' he learnt from his father – 'Oikonomia'. He has a penchant for bargain-basement suits, and became known as the 'Green Line Governor', a reference to the subway route he insists on taking to his Boston office. He jokes that he has already worked out which subway stop is nearest to the White House. This image is doubtless encouraged to dispel fears of his being a big-spending liberal but there is no doubt that he is much more prudent than his wife. A White House under the regime of First Lady Kitty would certainly be an interesting prospect.

None the less their differences seem to enhance their relationship rather than threaten it. It has led to speculation that there is an unfulfilled side to Michael Dukakis which his stoic self will only allow to be satisfied by vicarious pleasures. It may simply be that the Governor enjoys surrounding himself with people who do not agree with him on every subject – which could account for his choice of Senator Bentsen as a running partner. Perhaps Dukakis's greatest bonus at this stage of the presidential race is that he is not George Bush. For all those seeking a change from the Reagan legacy, the only choice now is Michael Dukakis. If he is elected, we shall see if the Democratic mule can take the lead when there is no one else holding the reins.

Lloyd Bentsen

BORN: 11 February 1921, Mission, Texas.

PARENTS: Father: Lloyd Millard Bentsen, entrepreneur in real estate, farming, oil and banking. Mother: Edna Ruth 'Dolly' (Colbath).

MARRIED: Beryl Ann 'B.A.' Longino, November 1943. Three children: Lloyd III, 43; Lan, 40; and Tina, 36.

EDUCATION: Graduated in Law from University of Texas, 1942.

MILITARY SERVICE: US Army Air Corps 1942–5. Left at rank of Major. Awarded Distinguished Flying Cross and Air Medal with three oak-leaf clusters.

CAREER: 1946–48 Judge, Hildago County, Texas.

1949–54 Congressman for Texas, serving three terms.

1955–70 President of Lincoln Consolidated (financial holdings), Houston.

1970 Elected Senator for Texas. Position still held.

1976 Stood for election as presidential candidate for the Democratic Party – beaten by Jimmy Carter.

In the same way as he has done with his marriage, Dukakis seems to have leashed himself to a polar opposite by selecting Lloyd Bentsen for his vice-presidential running mate. At first glance, the tall, well-dressed, millionaire Senator appears to have more in common with George Bush than with the short, earnest son of Greek immigrants who picked him to share the ticket. But there are clearly identifiable motives for the choice.

The so-called 'Boston–Austin' formula of a Massachusetts presidential candidate and a Texan 'veep' has had its successes; Dukakis was keen to draw comparisons with John F. Kennedy and Lyndon Johnson. The idea is to unite the diverse elements in the Democratic camp by combining a northern liberal with a southern conservative.

The state of Texas itself is important to Dukakis's campaign and it is clear that he is hoping Bentsen can carry it. Texas is the third-largest state in the Electoral College, carrying 29 electoral votes behind California's 47 and New York's 36. Dukakis comfortably leads the polls in the two larger states. Victory in all three would virtually guarantee him the presidency. The last Democrat to reach the White House without Texas was elected in 1844, before it became a state.

It would also be a great blow to George Bush to lose his nominated 'home' state. There is no guarantee, of course, that this will occur. Bush says the Texans would prefer a president to a vice-president. But Bentsen succeeded in beating him in the 1970 Texas senatorial elections and has held the seat ever since.

Because of a constitutional peculiarity he will be campaigning for re-election to his Senate seat at the same time as running his vice-presidential campaign. He cannot withdraw from the senatorial race at this late stage or the election will go to his Republican opponent by default. If he is elected into both positions he will automatically lose the Senate seat and Republican Governor William Clements will pick a replacement or order a special election. The dual campaign will certainly keep Bentsen in the public eye in Texas but it remains to be seen whether he can bring Dukakis the state and any of its southern neighbours.

Whatever advantages Bentsen brings, he is certainly no soul-mate to Dukakis. His background is affluent and patrician. His father, Lloyd senior, the son of Danish immigrants, came from South Dakota to marry a girl he had met in Mission. He settled and, with his brother, made a fortune by selling real estate to settlers from the north. Lloyd junior was born 11 February 1921 and grew up in the Rio Grande. He played with the children of Mexican immigrant labourers and learned fluent Spanish – one of the features he shares with Dukakis. He attended the University of Texas in Austin and graduated from the law school in 1942.

Enlisting in the army he was soon posted abroad, but returned to marry Texas model B.A. Longino. During the war he flew bombing missions over Europe and was decorated after being shot down twice.

On his return the war hero was elected the youngest judge in Texas at the age of 24. Two years later he was elected to Congress and befriended by the Speaker of the House, Texas Democrat Sam Rayburn. His three terms brought him experience but little recognition outside the House. He made one notorious speech in 1950 urging President Truman to drop an atom bomb on North Korea but says he is 'wiser now' whenever it is raised to cause him embarrassment.

By 1954, he had decided a congressman's salary was insufficient to raise three young children. He abandoned politics and with a $5 million loan from his family he started a life-insurance company which soon grew into a profitable corporate empire with interests in banking, real estate and oil fields.

Tiring of commercial success, he returned to the political arena in 1970, standing for senator against the Democratic incumbent Ralph Yarborough, whom he beat in a savage round of primary elections before going on to face George Bush as his Republican opponent. Victory gave him the senatorial seat he has held for the past 18 years. During this time he has become part of the Washington establishment.

Apart from one abortive attempt at the presidency in 1976 he has stuck to things he knows best, becoming a champion of business affairs and undoubtedly employing his own successful instincts. He earned the nickname of 'Loophole Lloyd' thanks to his mastery of tax policy and his ability to cut through the red tape associated with it. He also gained a reputation as an unsurpassed fundraiser, with the ability to mobilize his wealthy contacts whenever the cause required it.

Useful though his fiscal acumen might be to the present campaign, there are one or two inevitable questions about how well the conservative establishmentarian can get along with the inexperienced but idealistic presidential novice. Bentsen has brought in nearly $1.5 million in PAC contributions to the 1988 war chest. Dukakis refuses to accept anything from PACs.

Bentsen has travelled widely during his Senate years and has met many heads of state, which might, in part, compensate for Dukakis's inexperience in this field if it were not for the fact that the Senator loudly advocates a 'strong defence' including MX missiles and SDI, both of which Dukakis opposes.

There is nothing which says a president and his vice-president have to be ideological twins, and in many respects the diversity might broaden the appeal of their ticket across the political spectrum. But it must be clear who is leading and who is being led. With such imbalance of experience and ambition this might be a problem for the Dukakis–Bentsen ticket. Bentsen is the elder statesman in many ways, not least of all in age. He is the oldest vice-presidential nominee since Senator Alben Barkley in 1948, but then, as we have seen of late, the White House has no age limits for its residents.

THE REPUBLICANS

George Herbert Walker Bush

BORN:	12 June 1924, Milton, Massachusetts.
PARENTS:	Father: Prescott Sheldon Bush, stockbroker and Senator for Connecticut 1952–63. Mother: Dorothy (Walker).
MARRIED:	Barbara Pierce, January 1945. Five children: George, 41; Jeb, 35; Neil, 33; Marvin, 31; and Dorothy, 28.
EDUCATION:	Graduated in Economics from Yale, 1948. Phi Beta Kappa.
MILITARY SERVICE:	US Navy pilot, 1942–5. Left at rank of Lieutenant. Awarded Distinguished Flying Cross and three Air Medals.

CAREER:	
1948–50	Oil field supply salesman, Dresser Industries, Odessa, Texas.
1951	Bush–Overby Oil Development Co., co-founder.
1953	Zapata Petroleum Corp., co-founder.
1954	Zapata Off-shore Co., co-founder and president.
1964	Senatorial candidate for Texas – beaten by Ralph Yarborough.
1967–70	Congressman for Texas, serving two terms in the House of Representatives.
1970	Stood again in election of Senator for Texas – beaten by Lloyd Bentsen.
1971–73	Ambassador to the United Nations, appointed by President Nixon.
1973–74	Chairman, Republican National Committee.
1974–75	Chief of US Liaison Office in China, appointed by President Ford.
1976–77	Director, Central Intelligence Agency.
1977–79	Board member of various Houston corporate bodies.
1980–84	Stood for election as presidential candidate

for the Republican Party – beaten by Ronald Reagan. Nominated for vice-president by Reagan. Elected.

1985–   Both successfully re-elected in 1984.

Whether or not he was born to lead, George Bush was certainly born to succeed. His mother, Dorothy, was an heiress; his father, Prescott, a successful businessman who later became Republican senator for Connecticut. Prescott was working as an executive in a floorcovering company in Milton, Massachusetts, when George was born in 1924. Shortly afterwards the family transferred to New York where Bush senior prospered, eventually settling into a job as a Wall Street investment banker.

Young George knew little of the privation of the Depression years. His was a comfortable upbringing in Greenwich, Connecticut, with summers spent in Kennebunkport, Maine, where he still owns a holiday home. He was schooled privately at the fashionable Phillips Academy in Andover, Massachusetts and later followed in the footsteps of both his father and grandfather by going to Yale.

Some of his critics use this privileged background as a source of ammunition, claiming it divorces him from the experience of 'ordinary' Americans. But Bush will have none of it. His mother, Dorothy (known as 'Gam'), says that the late Senator Bush tried to instil a sense of duty in all their children: 'He was always telling them that because of your privileges, you also have responsibilities.' George Bush does not echo this specifically but he remembers 'A very close family, with a very strict disciplinarian of a father who mellowed in later years. He was a figure for whom everyone had respect and we children a certain awe.' He recalls his father as a natural leader who gave people a sense of purpose; obviously a model for his own aspirations.

But young George did not set out to follow the exact pattern of his father's successes. The war interrupted his schooling and, keen to serve his country, he enlisted as soon as he reached the age of 18, becoming the youngest pilot in the US Navy. On top of this achievement he managed a heroic escape when his plane was shot down over the Pacific, and other members of the crew were killed.

In 1945 a well-decorated Lieutenant Bush returned to Greenwich and married Barbara Pierce, daughter of McCall's publisher Marvin Pierce. After graduating in Economics from Yale, he decided, like all good American heroes, to make his fortune. Turning down a job in the investment business on Wall Street, he took a $375-a-month job as an oil-field supply salesman in Odessa, the driest and flattest part of west Texas. He did well in the oil business and by the age of 30 had become the millionaire president of his own off-shore drilling company, Zapata, named after the Mexican revolutionary.

Bush is proud of his business achievements, feeling he did it on his own without all the benefits of inherited wealth which he could easily have called upon. Perhaps this forms the basis of his fundamentally conservative approach to economics. He is a great believer in free enterprise and still an opponent of federal intervention in industry. His recent support of President Reagan's stand against the 60-day notification clause in the current Trade Bill may well bring him a lot of flak in this year's pre-election debates.

By 1963, having made his fortune, Bush decided it was time to do his duty and enter politics. He was elected as chairman of the Harris County (Houston) Republican Party and gained the nomination to stand for the 1964 senatorial elections in Texas but he was beaten by Democrat Ralph Yarborough. Undeterred, in 1966 he went on to win a congressional seat on Houston's affluent west side. Before taking office he sold his share in Zapata to avoid any conflict of interest. His career as a full-time politician had begun.

In his first term in the House he made a good impression on Richard Nixon, whose presidential nomination he supported in 1968. Not content with a second term as a congressman, in 1970 he tried once more for the Senate seat in Texas. This time he was facing a certain Lloyd Bentsen on the Democratic bench. Bentsen ran a somewhat conservative campaign, having beaten the Democratic incumbent for nomination (Yarborough) on anti-liberal issues. Indeed, Bush and Bentsen often seemed to have more in common with each other than with their own parties during early parts of the campaign but the battle eventually heated up, particularly when President Nixon and Vice-President Spiro Agnew weighed in with their support for Bush. In the long run it was Bentsen who triumphed. He is recorded as saying, some ten years later, during Bush's last attempt at the presidency, that he considered him 'a first-class gentleman who always campaigned on the issues with no impugning of motives'. He did add, however, that he doubted his potential as a president because 'It takes a little of the killer instinct, you know.'

Bush was far from deserted in defeat. Nixon offered him the post of ambassador to the United Nations, in spite of his lack of previous experience in diplomatic affairs. To the surprise of many of his peers, he executed the role with considerable efficacy and two years later, at the beginning of 1973, he bowed to the President's request to replace Robert Dole as chairman of the Republican National Committee. In a characteristic expression of loyalty to the Presidency, above all else, he told reporters 'When the President wants you to do something, in my kind of system of civics you ought to do it.' Ironically, it was a comment which was to imperil his credibility shortly afterwards.

When the scandal of Watergate broke, Bush must have found himself in one of the most unenviable positions ever. With the dice hopelessly loaded against him, his duty was as brave standard-bearer for the Republican Party, under the hostile scrutiny of the whole nation. He consistently supported the President, chastised the media and held firm while all crashed around him. It is said that in private he confided to a national commitee meeting in April 1974 that he had become 'plagued with doubts' but to the outside world he kept a diplomatic insistence that the President would do 'what is right, what is best for the country'.

Eventually (and, no doubt, to his relief), he found himself answering to a new president, and many expected that Gerald Ford would be likely to pick him as vice-president. But it was not to be: Nelson Rockefeller got the job. Instead, Bush found himself packing his bags to take up a new post as chief of the US Liaison Office in China. The following year, 1975, he was brought home again by Ford to take over as director of the Central Intelligence Agency.

Once again it was an unenviable lot. The CIA had been receiving an extremely bad press. Swathed in allegations of unscrupulous and often illegal activities, the Agency was low in morale and vulnerable to the point of having its very necessity questioned. In effect, Bush apologized for the past misdemeanours, promised they would not be repeated and insisted the Agency was absolutely vital to national security. He then set about implementing a series of unpublicized reforms with the result that confidence was restored and the Agency was perceived to be in better shape than it had been for many years.

When Jimmy Carter beat defending President Ford and took office in January 1977, Bush returned to Houston and briefly dabbled in business affairs, accepting directorships on the boards of assorted companies. But it was not long before he started looking forward to the 1980 presidential election and investigating the idea of standing for nomination himself.

He filed his papers in January 1979 and under the auspices of Jim Baker (who is back managing his team this year), began a committed campaign. He rejected any suggestion that he might accept nomination for vice-president, convinced that his previous experience made him a better man for the Number One job than the favourite, Ronald Reagan. Asked why, he replied 'I have this quiet conviction that I'd know just how to handle the Presidency the day I took the oath of office. I would just know how to do it and I'd do it with class. ... You don't have to fit a mould to be classy, and there are all different kinds of class. I think I've got it. ... Somehow, if I go the extra mile, the system will work and I'll prevail over Reagan because it's right that I prevail. I have a perception of the world that Reagan doesn't have.'

Despite a determined fight (he beat Reagan in the Iowa caucuses) and after a $16 million campaign, he was still not getting the recognition he needed to make it through to nomination. Baker advised that a strategic withdrawal would pay off with Reagan's selection for the vice-presidential slot. Bush swallowed his pride, resigned himself to 'voodoo economics' and was duly rewarded with second prize.

He may now be wondering whether he should ever have accepted the trophy. If he makes it to the Oval Office this time round, he has promised a place on the wall to Martin Van Buren. Van Buren was the last vice-president later to be elected president in his own right – and that was in 1836. History and early opinion poll results seem stacked against Bush, though there could scarcely be anyone with better qualifications.

Apart from all the public positions he has held, he has travelled to more than 70 countries during his time as Vice-President; he holds 21 honorary degrees; and he has actually acted as President before – albeit, only for a few hours whilst Reagan underwent surgery in July 1985. He has served in an administration which closes with lower interest rates, lower unemployment figures and a more peaceful international environment than when it began. So why should it be such an uphill struggle?

Basically, a vice-president's lot is not a happy one: traditionally it is said to be 'not worth a bucket of spit'. Bush is quoted as saying, 'You sublimate your own priorities and your own passions for a team': yet he has made more of an impression than many of his predecessors. Now it's his turn to step out into the spotlight and he is in danger of being eclipsed. His loyalty to the President remains firm: he refuses to cite any of the administration's mistakes, claiming it is a matter of honour and decency not to do so.

Supporting such a popular president might be thought a shrewd measure but, on the other hand, Bush's total steadfastness has led to him being tagged as a yes-man, possessed of nothing of his own but the much-quoted 'wimp'-factor. He is well aware of the problem and says he will take half the blame for anything that went wrong in the past eight years if he gets a fraction of the credit for what went right but, of course, things don't work that way. A president's successes are his own; alas, his blunders are a legacy.

The Iran–Contra affair is a particularly haunting skeleton which seems unlikely to rest even though the pending trials have been postponed until after the election. If Bush knew about the transactions, he is lying by denying it now, say his detractors. If he, as former Director of the CIA, had no knowledge of what was going on, doubt must be cast on his competence as an adviser to the President, let alone his suitability for the job himself. He was only just saved from the embarrassment of one of Reagan's other skeletons when Ed Meese made a timely resignation in July. Had he remained, Bush would have been faced with extremely difficult questions about whether or not he intended to fire the controversial Attorney-General.

It is true that if he survives such controversies with a totally untarnished reputation, it is a credit to his personal integrity. But at best, it suggests that his much vaunted experience has failed to teach him how to assess what is going on around him.

His other major difficulty is his public image. Those who know him personally often describe a loyal, energetic, warm man with a winning sense of humour and great strength of character. But this fails to translate to the public at large. Perhaps one of the reasons he seems devoid of a strong identity is that he tries too hard to please everyone. As a result, facts are blurred: where he comes from (Texas? Massachusetts? Maine?), what his policies are, and so on; all seem woolly and vague. He says he wants to be an 'education' president, but does not clarify what that entails. He vows not to raise taxes but has not explained, so far, how he will clear the nation's record budget deficit. His language often unwittingly works against him as well. He tends to come out with boyish, preppy phrases such as 'golly' and 'all that stuff', and has been known to refer to metaphorical political excrement as 'deep doo-doo'. Unlike Reagan, he lacks the charisma to pass off the endless gaffes.

When he does make an effort to shrug the 'wimp' label it often backfires on him. In a rare live television conflict early this year, he railed against interviewer Dan Rather's continued probing about his role in the Iran–Contra affair. After the event, viewers answering opinion polls said that whilst they did think Bush had been rudely goaded, he still came across as having something to hide. It seems he simply picked the wrong topic on which to take a stand.

Polls also show he lacks appeal to the female vote. Some suggest this relates to his stand against abortion and other welfare issues which strongly influence women. Others suggest that his relationship with his wife Barbara could be more cordial. Still more suggest that he just does not cut enough of a dash with the ladies.

George Bush says he does not take too much notice of the image-makers; he fights better as the underdog. Besides he is far more concerned with the features he thinks are really important in a President. He lists these as 'integrity', 'experience to make intelligent decisions', and the ability to 'command respect'. If only he could convince the nation this is what he is offering, it might make all the difference.

In 1979, when he last stood as presidential candidate, the *Washington Post* said of Bush: 'In a Reagan-less world, his chances might look pretty good.' As Reagan takes his curtain calls, we shall surely find out if they were right.

James Danforth Quayle

BORN:	4 February 1947, Indianapolis, Indiana.
PARENTS:	Father: James C. Quayle, publisher; Mother: Corinne (Pulliam).
MARRIED:	Marilyn Tucker, November 1972. Three children: Tucker, 14; Benjamin, 12; and Corinne, 10.
EDUCATION:	Graduated in Political Science from DePauw University, 1969. Gained his JD from Indiana University School of Law, 1974.
MILITARY SERVICE:	Served in the Indiana National Guard 1969–75.
CAREER: 1974–76	Attorney and associate publisher of Huntingdon Herald Press.
1977–80	Congressman for two terms.
1981	Elected Senator for Indiana.
1986	Re-elected to Senate to serve until 1992.

When Senator Dan Quayle's name first sprang to George Bush's lips as the long-awaited vice-presidential nominee, some onlookers declared the choice perplexing and surprising. It may have seemed that way to the young Indiana Senator himself; it is said that a month before the New Orleans convention he was not even planning to attend.

Bush seemed determined to make it plain that the decision was his alone. He methodically telephoned the other possible contenders to advise them they had not been selected, thus avoiding the disunity which emerged when Dukakis failed to contact Jackson about the Democratic vice-presidential nomination. As the front-runners publicly declared that they had been eliminated it became clear that the position had gone to an outsider in the field and speculation about Quayle prompted Bush to make an early announcement rather than allow the press to pre-empt his coup.

As the news sank in, the pundits' appraisals varied widely. Many deduced that every coin of good fortune Quayle brought to the ticket seemed tarnished on the flipside.

At 41, his youth brought 'father and son' appeal, they declared. He would attract fellow 'baby-boomers' (post-war babies – a large proportion of the voting population – though there is no evidence that they vote for their own age group). Bush would seem the competent patriarchal statesman beside him. On the other hand, his experience seemed minimal for a post frequently described as being 'a heartbeat away' from the presidency.

He was hailed as an asset in attracting women voters who had previously shown antipathy towards Bush but who might be wooed by the allegedly 'good-looking' Senator. At the same time it was speculated that he might widen the gender gap by alienating women with his anti-abortion stand.

Quayle was seen by some as being a Bush clone. He was born into a wealthy publishing family in Indianapolis. His maternal grandfather was Eugene C. Pulliam, the multi-millionaire publisher of a large newspaper chain, who had a reputation for extreme right-wing views. Quayle stands to inherit a large sum from the Pulliam estate although he has been at pains to point out that he and his family live only 'comfortably' at the moment.

After graduating in political science from DePauw University in 1969, Quayle studied law at Indiana University and was admitted to the Bar in 1974. During this time he was chief investigator for the Consumer Protection Division of the Indiana Attorney-General's Office between 1970 and 1971; administrative assistant to Governor Edgar Whitcomb from 1971 to 1973; and director of the Inheritance Tax Division of the Indiana Department of Revenue from 1973 to 1974.

The most controversial aspect of this period in his life was his service in the Indiana National Guard (almost an American equivalent of the Territorial Army). Critics claim he used family influence to opt out of the Vietnam draft. Quayle insists he was simply trying to study for his law degree whilst serving his country on the home front.

In 1972 he met Marilyn Tucker at law school. Attraction was instant and they married ten weeks later. She also went on to qualify as a lawyer.

Quayle joined the family business in 1974 and worked as an associate publisher there until 1977 when he entered Congress. His service in the House appears to have been generally unremarkable.

In 1980 he became the youngest-ever Senator for Indiana at the age of 33. He promised 'A New Generation of Leadership' and succeeded in snatching the Senate seat Birch Bayh had occupied for eighteen years. Despite a minor scandal when it was revealed that, during his time in the House, Quayle had spent a weekend in the company of pin-up lobbyist Paula Parkinson and two other congressmen, he was cleared of any impropriety and his popularity held. In 1986 he was swept back into office with a record 61% margin. He found favour with the conservative right wing of the

Republican Party and his voting record in the Senate shows that, for about 80% of the time, he has supported President Reagan's position on issues.

The three major committees on which he has served during his Senate tenure reflect the nature of his major policy concerns: the Armed Services Committee, the Budget Committee, and the Labor and Human Relations Committee. In his first term he headed a task force and sub-committee which investigated Pentagon procurement (there had been allegations of corruption in the way in which ex-Pentagon officials headed companies tendering for multi-million-dollar defence contracts). As a result of the sub-committee's efforts the law was tightened up and more competitive tenders were encouraged.

His policy on foreign and defence issues is conservative down the line. He is for Contra Aid, deployment of SDI and what he calls 'the strengthening of US defense capabilities'. On the Budget Committee he voted against a military spending freeze although he had previously voiced doubts over the large defence spending increases favoured by Casper Weinberger.

On labour and social issues he appears more of a moderate compared with the ultra-conservative element. He chaired a sub-committee on job programmes which prevented their total demise by encouraging private business to become involved in them, rather than their depending entirely on local government funding. He also championed a proposal to simplify tax returns, reducing them, on average, to the size of a postcard.

Above all, he is seen as a team player in the Senate and perhaps this was what attracted George Bush most. Having stood so long in the shadow of President Reagan, he must have been keen to find a loyal vice-president of his own who would follow his lead without detracting from the presidential role. Quayle's style of oratory is more compelling than Bush's and his vitality may serve the campaign well in the debates but he is not likely to deviate substantially from any of Bush's policies as a more established running mate might have done.

It seems that personal qualities played a major role in Bush's choice; in geographic terms Quayle brings nothing to the ticket. Indiana is one of the safest Republican states in the Union and it carries only 12 votes in the Electoral College. Whilst the Democrats have been gaining a little ground in the Midwest recently, it is not an area which Bush needed to guarantee.

Only the election in November can resolve the debate over whether George Bush made the right choice. If he did, Dan Quayle will become the third-youngest vice-president in US history.

CHAPTER SIX

The Changing Political Map of the United States

One of the keys to understanding the politics of the United States is the recognition of the sheer size of the country and how this has shaped its history and development. The US is so large that in travelling from its east to west coasts you cross three time zones. Indeed, London is nearer to Cairo than New York is to San Francisco. Although the analogy is far from perfect, one might view the US as being made up of a series of European nation states.

In order to try to understand this vast country we have divided it into four regions: East, Midwest, South and West. In this chapter the significant changes which have taken place both within and between them are monitored. A series of five standard tables is presented for each of the four regions, to illustrate some of the changes which have occurred between 1944 and 1984.

Firstly, the changing balance of population within and between the regions is reviewed in the five appropriate census years: 1940, 1950, 1960, 1970 and 1980. The US census began in 1790 and has been repeated every ten years thereafter. Its most immediate political significance stems from the fact that the number of representatives (congressmen) each state is entitled to send to Washington is determined by its share of the national population as recorded in the census. Americans are already discussing the likely consequences of the 1990 census: which states will gain seats and which will lose them. This in turn has consequences (as Chapter Three explains) for the allocation of electoral college votes among the states (given that the number of electoral college votes is equivalent to the number of senators and representatives each state sends to Washington).

Secondly, the share of the total vote gained by the Democrats and Republicans in the region for the eleven presidential elections between 1944 and 1984 is shown. This offers a broad indication of the strengths of the parties over the period and reveals, for instance, the Democratic strength in the East and the Republican strength in the West.

Thirdly, a slightly more complex table, a variation of the one described immediately above, records the share which each region contributed to the national vote for the Democrats and Republicans in those same elections. Thus, for example, the Democrats secured 51.8% of the East's votes in 1944 and this represented 33.5% of the party's national vote that year.

Fourthly, the number of times each state in the region has voted Democrat or Republican between 1944 and 1984 is tabulated. This standard table is divided into two columns: 1944–64 (six elections) and 1968–84 (five elections). The 1944–64 period was dominated by the Democrats who won four out of the six elections and it ended with Lyndon Johnson's landslide victory for the Democrats in 1964. However, four out of five elections in the second period, 1968–84, were won by the Republicans.

Finally, the number of senators, representatives and governors for both parties in the region following the last mid-term elections, in 1986, is listed. What may surprise is that the tally of Democrats in all three groups is much greater than recent presidential voting in all the regions would suggest. In Chapter Two we set out some of the reasons for this apparent discrepancy in voting behaviour. But one other factor is the propensity of American voters to 'split their ticket' – to vote, say, for Republican presidential and senate candidates and for Democratic candidates for the House of Representatives and governor, *all at the same time*. This 'vote splitting' has always occurred but it is even more common nowadays as party loyalties decline. In addition, because so much of US politics is very localized, many voters do judge candidates by their record rather than by their party label. For example, New Jersey has voted Republican in all of the last five presidential elections but, currently, both of its senators are Democrats, as are eight of its fourteen representatives. Its governor is a Republican and he faces a state Senate controlled by the Democrats and a state House narrowly controlled by the Republicans.

THE EAST

For more than 150 years this was the gateway to the US for successive waves of immigrants. Many of them stayed in the region, working in city sweat shops or in the major manufacturing industries which dominated its economy. But it is a region of contrasts: the dense urban concentrations of New York and Pennsylvania co-exist with the suburban sprawl of Connecticut and Maryland and the rural calm of Maine and Vermont.

The real growth years for population in recent times were 1940–70, as the table below shows:

Census year	Population	% increase
1940	38,727,000	
1950	42,941,000	+10.9
1960	48,988,000	+14.1
1970	54,290,000	+10.8
1980	54,585,000	+ 0.5

In the 1970s, the traditional low-wage jobs which had underpinned the region's economy began to disappear to the non-unionised South and West at an accelerating rate. They were followed by an exodus of population. The metropolitan area of New York lost almost 5% of its population between 1970 and 1980. In the 1980s a pattern of cross-migration developed: people with lower incomes, fewer skills and less education continued to move out as skilled people moved in to take advantage of the recent growth in high-income, high-technology employment. These higher-income groups have given a more Republican tinge to a traditionally more Democratic region.

The region's tradition of high taxation to finance substantial public services took a heavy pounding in the 1970s, culminating in New York City's near bankruptcy in 1975. The reaction to these events led to substantial cuts in state and local taxes and a much greater emphasis on financing services through economic growth.

Politically, the significance of the region has been declining since the war. While its population has grown for most of the period, its rate of growth has been surpassed in other regions (most particularly by the West). In the 1944 election it accounted for 149 electoral college votes. This figure fell slightly to 145 in 1952, to 142 in 1964 and to 138 in 1972. However, by 1984 it had fallen to 129 and some estimates for the reapportionment which will automatically follow the 1990 census suggest that the region may lose another six or more. New York and Pennsylvania account for the greatest part of the loss: in 1944 they represented 47 and 35 electoral college votes respectively; but by 1984 these had been reduced to 36 and 25.

THE EAST

MAINE

VERMONT

NEW HAMPSHIRE

MASSACHUSETTS

RHODE ISLAND

CONNECTICUT

NEW YORK

NEW JERSEY

DELAWARE

MARYLAND

(Part of Virginia)

PENNSYLVANIA

DISTRICT OF COLUMBIA

The regional division of votes between the two main parties in recent presidential elections is set out below:

Presidential election	Democrat %	Republican %
1944	**51.8**	47.8
1948	47.2	**47.9**
1952	44.2	**55.1**
1956	39.1	**60.6**
1960	**52.7**	47.0
1964	**68.2**	31.5
1968	**50.0**	42.8
1972	41.5	**57.5**
1976	**51.2**	47.2
1980	42.4	**47.1**
1984	44.7	**54.8**

Since John F. Kennedy's election in 1960 the region has voted more Democrat than the nation as a whole (most markedly in 1964 when it resoundingly rejected Barry Goldwater). However, when we look at what percentage the region's votes represent of the total national votes cast for each party over the same period we see a marked decline in the contribution it makes to both parties, since 1944:

Regional share of national party vote		
Presidential election	Democrat %	Republican %
1944	33.5	35.9
1948	32.4	36.1
1952	32.1	32.3
1956	29.9	33.9
1960	32.8	29.4
1964	33.4	24.5
1968	33.3	28.1
1972	30.8	26.5
1976	26.8	25.8
1980	25.3	22.7
1984	26.9	22.8

In 1944 the region accounted for one-third or more of the national vote for both parties. By 1984 this was reduced to one-quarter of the Democratic vote and just over one-fifth of the Republican.

Looking at how many times each state in the region has voted Democrat or Republican in the last eleven presidential elections we can see how Democrat Lyndon Johnson's overwhelming victory in 1964 marks a dividing line. The very scale of his victory over Goldwater (who won none of the states in the East) simply points up the degree of shift to the Republicans in most of the subsequent elections:

| | 1944–64 | | 1968–84 | |
	Dem	Rep	Dem	Rep
Connecticut	3	3	1	4
Delaware	3	3	1	4
District of Columbia (a)	1	0	5	0
Maine	1	5	1	4
Maryland	3	3	3	2
Massachusetts	4	2	3	2
New Hampshire	2	4	0	5
New Jersey	3	3	0	5
New York	3	3	2	3
Pennsylvania	3	3	2	3
Rhode Island	4	2	3	2
Vermont	1	5	0	5

Note: (a) First voted in presidential elections in 1964

The period to 1964 is much more balanced than 1968 onwards. The Democrats have fared better in the East than elsewhere in the country but the big state of New Jersey and the smaller states of Connecticut, Delaware and New Hampshire have moved solidly into the Republican camp in the last five presidential elections.

Following the mid-term elections in 1986, the region's party representation was as follows:

	Democrat	Republican
Senate	12	10
House	62	42
Governors	6	5

Elections for senators and governors involve the entire electorate in any state and here the Democrats only narrowly lead. Elections to the House are based upon one representative per district. Each state is divided into a number of districts equal to its entitlement of representatives. Thus, in the small state of Delaware, with only one representative, the entire electorate of the state was engaged in voting for him. However, the large state of New York is divided into 34 districts, each returning one representative. It is in these smaller, local areas where the Democrats generally perform significantly better than their state-wide presidential vote would suggest.

THE MIDWEST

This region combines the farm belt of the United States in the Great Plains with industrial states clustered round the Great Lakes in the north. Its population growth, as in the East, faltered in the 1970s:

Census year	Population	% increase
1940	40,144,000	
1950	44,462,000	+10.8
1960	51,619,000	+16.0
1970	56,589,000	+ 9.6
1980	58,868,000	+ 4.0

The region has had considerable problems in recent years. Farming has ceased to be a major employer in the US and in the Great Plains area less than 10% of the population are now farmers. But agriculture is still a crucial component in the regional economy. In the 1970s farming experienced a great boom and many farmers borrowed heavily to take full advantage of the expansion and of the consequent increase in land prices. The US Department of Agriculture Index of average value per acre (taking 1977 as 100) registered 42 in 1970, 125 in 1979, rising to 158 in 1981. But by 1987 it had slumped to 103. Total farm debt in the US rose from $53 billion in 1970 to $195 billion in 1981. The slump in the 1980s caused a succession of bankruptcies. 1987 brought some relief to the farmers as cereal exports increased substantially but this year's drought has set them back again with federal emergencies declared in 30 states.

The industrial states in the north have also faced lean times in recent years. The two staple industries of car and steel manufacturing shed large numbers of jobs and introduced wage cuts for remaining employees. The consequences were quite dramatic: between 1970 and 1986, Detroit lost 28% of its population and Cleveland lost 27%. However, after much painful adjustment, the region shows some signs of revival. Chicago has compensated for losses in its traditional industries by a growth in white-collar jobs. Other areas have followed a similar path, adapting to both high-technology and low-wage industries.

Politically, like the East, its significance has declined. In 1944 it accounted for 155 electoral college votes. This number fell to 153 in 1952, 149 in 1964 and 145 in 1972. By 1984 it had fallen further to 137 and estimates of reapportionment after the 1990 census suggest that the region may lose another six or seven votes.

The regional division of votes between the two main parties in recent presidential elections is as follows:

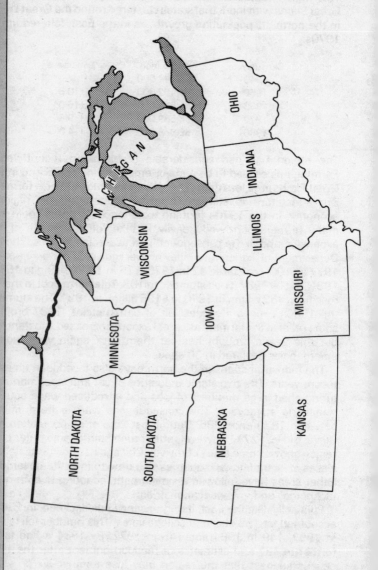

THE MIDWEST

OHIO

INDIANA

ILLINOIS

MISSOURI

MICHIGAN

WISCONSIN

MINNESOTA

IOWA

NORTH DAKOTA

SOUTH DAKOTA

NEBRASKA

KANSAS

Presidential election	Democrat %	Republican %
1944	49.2	**50.4**
1948	**50.3**	48.0
1952	42.0	**57.6**
1956	41.2	**58.6**
1960	47.6	**52.2**
1964	**61.4**	38.5
1968	43.7	**46.8**
1972	39.4	**59.1**
1976	48.3	**49.7**
1980	40.9	**50.9**
1984	41.3	**58.0**

In the last eleven elections the Midwest has given the Republicans less than 50% in only four. Even the nadir of Republican post-war fortunes in 1964 saw nearly 40% of voters supporting Barry Goldwater. To a degree the region has become less significant to the Republicans nationally as shown in their share of the national vote for the party:

Regional share of national party vote		
Presidential election	Democrat %	Republican %
1944	34.4	41.0
1948	36.6	38.3
1952	32.5	35.9
1956	33.4	34.8
1960	32.0	35.2
1964	31.6	31.5
1968	31.0	32.7
1972	31.3	29.1
1976	28.6	30.6
1980	29.0	29.2
1984	28.0	27.1

On the surface it appears that the Democrats have survived far better than the Republicans in this traditionally Republican region. But the declining share of the national Republican vote is due to the increase in the total Republican vote in the other regions of the country.

Looking at how the states in the region voted in the period 1944–84 we can easily see what an obstacle course it presents to Michael Dukakis this year:

	1944–64		1968–84	
	Dem	Rep	Dem	Rep
Illinois	4	2	0	5
Indiana	1	5	0	5
Iowa	2	4	0	5
Kansas	1	5	0	5
Michigan	3	3	1	4
Minnesota	4	2	4	1
Missouri	5	1	1	4
Nebraska	1	5	0	5
North Dakota	1	5	0	5
Ohio	2	4	1	4
South Dakota	1	5	0	5
Wisconsin	2	4	1	4

In the five presidential elections since 1968 the Democrats have not once carried seven of the region's twelve states and four of the remaining five they have only carried once. Since 1968, there seems to have been little difference in presidential voting patterns between the industrial and farming states within the region. From 1968, Michigan has voted Republican four times out of five and Illinois five out of five. Only Minnesota, home of the Democratic-Farmer-Labor Party (DFL), Hubert Humphrey, and Walter Mondale has bucked the regional trend in recent years.

Following the mid-term elections of 1986, the region's party representation was as follows:

	Democrat	Republican
Senate	11	13
House	62	51
Governors	4	8

The Republicans hold a narrow advantage in Senate representation but a two-to-one advantage among the region's governors. However, in the House contests it is the Democrats who hold a small but respectable lead.

THE SOUTH

This region has faced the most profound changes of all four, both economically and politically. It combines the oil wealth of Texas and the industrial expansion of the Atlantic seaboard states with the continuing poverty of the states flanking the Mississippi.

Overall growth in population has been steady since 1940, but accelerated in the 1970s:

Census year	Population	% increase
1940	38,916,000	
1950	43,736,000	+12.4
1960	50,662,000	+15.8
1970	57,583,000	+13.7
1980	69,923,000	+21.4

These figures conceal a more complex picture. Between 1940 and 1980, 50.5% of the region's population growth was accounted for by only two states – Florida and Texas. Whilst the population of the region as a whole grew by 80% over this same period, the populations of Kentucky and Oklahoma each grew by only 29%, the population of Arkansas by 17%, Mississippi by 15% and West Virginia by 3%.

The greatest change in population trends in the South was the rapid decline, in the 1970s, of the traditionally enormous migration from the region of blacks seeking both employment and an escape from the oppressive regime of racial segregation which existed in so many southern states. As the campaign for civil rights in the 1960s began to take hold and institutionalized segregation was dismantled, economically active blacks stayed in the South. At the same time investors, who had previously shunned the region, began to look favourably on the South with its non-unionised, low-wage economy. The 'New South' became a commonplace description of these changes, conjuring up the picture of a region fast turning away from its old and divisive Dixie past, changing its ways and embracing economic growth.

The Atlantic seaboard states have enjoyed spectacular growth in recent years. Florida has quadrupled its population since 1940, as the elderly have poured in either to settle permanently or to stay for the long winter months. North Carolina became the tenth most populous state in the Union in 1980 with its mixture of new high-technology industries developing alongside the more traditional textile, furniture and tobacco industries. Atlanta, in Georgia, has also boomed.

In the oil belt, to the west of the region, OPEC's quadrupling of oil prices in the early 1970s must have seemed designed by heaven with Louisiana, Oklahoma and Texas in mind. By the early 1980s

THE SOUTH

Map of the Southern United States showing: WEST VIRGINIA, VIRGINIA, NORTH CAROLINA, SOUTH CAROLINA, FLORIDA, GEORGIA, KENTUCKY, TENNESSEE, ALABAMA, MISSISSIPPI, ARKANSAS, LOUISIANA, OKLAHOMA, TEXAS these states were among the fastest growing in the country. But the subsequent collapse in oil prices has brought correspondingly serious problems to their economies.

The states along the Mississippi valley have not shared the same degree of prosperity as the rest of the region. Incomes have improved, but they still lag far behind the national average. Alabama has not compensated for the loss of its steel industry, Arkansas is struggling and Mississippi still has one of the weakest economies in the country.

Overall, in terms of electoral college votes, the region has remained fairly stable. In 1944 it accounted for 156 votes, falling to 154 in 1952 and 152 in 1964. By 1972 it had gained one vote, and jumped to 161 by 1984. But these overall figures disguise shifts within the region: eight states had fewer votes in 1984 than in 1944, whereas Florida shot up from 8 votes in 1944 to 21 in 1984. Over the same period the number of electoral college votes for Texas rose from 23 to 29. Estimates of reapportionment for the 1990s suggest a gain of between five and ten votes for the region.

The regional division of votes between the two main parties in recent elections is set out below:

Presidential election	Democrat %	Republican %
1944	66.2	31.6
1948	52.8	30.8
1952	51.1	48.8
1956	47.2	50.3
1960	49.6	47.6
1964	51.9	46.6
1968	32.2	36.1
1972	29.3	69.2
1976	53.9	44.9
1980	44.4	51.6
1984	37.2	62.3

What a remarkable story unfolds: the Democratic hegemony of 1944 has been broken and replaced by Republican dominance for three out of the last four presidential elections. The first earthquake on the political Richter Scale came in 1948 when a number of southern states, objecting to the growing campaign for civil rights within the Democratic Party, supported their own 'States Rights' candidate who carried four states in the election. In 1964 Barry Goldwater carried only six states and, apart from his own native Arizona, they all came from the South. In 1968, George Wallace of Alabama stood as an Independent and carried five southern states, arguably robbing the Democrats of national victory. In 1972, the Democratic candidate, George McGovern, epitomized everything the southern conservative Democrats loathed about liberal politicians and Richard Nixon swept the region with a vote which is still the high-water mark for the Republicans this century. We see the true measure of the change when we look at the region's share of the national party vote:

Presidential election	Democrat %	Republican %
Regional share of national party vote		
1944	18.2	10.1
1948	16.2	10.4
1952	21.3	16.3
1956	20.6	16.0
1960	19.0	18.3
1964	19.1	25.9
1968	18.1	19.9
1972	18.4	26.8
1976	28.2	24.5
1980	29.9	28.0
1984	26.4	30.5

Comparing 1944 with 1984, the South's share of the national Democratic vote has increased by 8%, but its share of the Republican vote has increased by 20%. Over the period the composition of the Democratic vote has changed: it now has a very significant black element. The Republican vote has also changed: it has been swollen by disaffected white Democrats as well as by middle-class immigrants seeking retirement or high incomes from the region's new prosperity.

The table opposite reveals the political turmoil of the region by setting out how each state voted throughout the period 1944–84:

	1944–64		1968–84	
	Dem	Rep	Dem	Rep
Alabama (a,b)	4	1	1	3
Arkansas (b)	6	0	1	3
Florida	3	3	1	4
Georgia (b)	5	1	2	2
Kentucky	4	2	1	4
Louisiana (a,b)	3	2	1	3
Mississippi (a,b,c)	3	1	2	2
North Carolina	6	0	1	4
Oklahoma	3	3	0	5
South Carolina (a)	4	1	1	4
Tennessee	3	3	1	4
Texas	4	2	2	3
Virginia	3	3	0	5
West Virginia	5	1	3	2

Notes: (a) States Rights candidate in 1948
     (b) George Wallace in 1968
     (c) Unpledged delegation in 1960

If Georgia's Jimmy Carter had not won the Democratic nomination in 1976, the party's 1968–84 column would probably look even sorrier.

However, at state level, the Republican advance in the South, whilst still impressive, is far less complete. Following the mid-term elections in 1986, the region's party representation was as follows:

	Democrat	Republican
Senate	20	8
House	89	44
Governors	7	7

This dramatic political inversion of fortunes, comparing presidential elections with those for the Senate and House, is the most extraordinary in any of the four regions. Many Democratic candidates are returned because of the overwhelming support for the party among black voters in the South. But whites will also vote for Democratic candidates who represent, to them, the traditional conservative values that once made Dixie synonymous with Democrat.

THE WEST

MONTANA

WYOMING

COLORADO

NEW MEXICO

UTAH

ARIZONA

IDAHO

NEVADA

WASHINGTON

OREGON

CALIFORNIA

ALASKA

HAWAII

THE WEST

The West is undoubtedly the boom region of the US, but its population distribution is highly imbalanced. The enormous mountain and desert states are inhabited by relatively few people, many of whom are clustered round vital water sources. Yet California has not only the largest population of any state in the Union but also the most urbanized (91.3% according to the 1980 census). The region's population growth has been meteoric – trebling between 1940 and 1980, as the table below shows:

Census year	Population	% increase
1940	14,378,000	
1950	20,191,000	+40.4
1960	28,053,000	+38.9
1970	34,838,000	+24.2
1980	43,173,000	+23.9

All but three states in the region have at least doubled their population size. California dominates the whole area. It alone accounts for 58% of the region's increase in population over the period; and, in 1980, contained 55% of the entire regional population.

Wealthy Americans and poor immigrants alike have poured into California. Both groups were attracted by its booming economy but the former also sought the climate and environment which the state offers. It has an intensive and prosperous agriculture, as well as the most highly developed high-technology economy anywhere in the world. Ex-Governor Ronald Reagan used to boast that if California were an independent country it would have the seventh-largest gross national product in the world. But, in Los Angeles, affluence sits side by side with violent street gangs and drug trafficking. To the north, in Washington State, an economy based upon timber and Boeing has been hit by the problems of both. To the east, both Nevada and Utah have grown significantly in population. They share a border but very little else: the former is the gambling centre of the US whilst the latter is a state built by Mormons.

The region has also grown greatly in political significance. In 1944 it accounted for only 71 electoral college votes. This figure increased to 79 in 1952, to 95 by 1964 and 102 by 1972. By 1984 the number of votes in the region amounted to 111. Likely reapportionment in the 1990s suggests a gain of between five and seven votes.

The regional division of votes between the two main parties in recent elections is set out overleaf:

Presidential election	Democrat %	Republican %
1944	**55.2**	44.2
1948	**49.4**	46.3
1952	41.9	**57.3**
1956	43.3	**56.3**
1960	48.5	**51.1**
1964	**59.4**	40.4
1968	43.7	**48.7**
1972	39.0	**57.1**
1976	45.7	**51.0**
1980	34.4	**54.0**
1984	39.2	**59.6**

The Republicans have received less than 50% of the regional vote in only four out of the eleven presidential elections in the period. The nadir of Democratic fortunes was Jimmy Carter's defeat in 1980, when an unpopular President fought a Republican from California. Their recovery in 1984 only put them fractionally ahead of George McGovern's poor performance in 1972.

Looking at the region's share of the national party vote one is struck by the relative stability throughout the period:

Regional share of national party vote

Presidential election	Democrat %	Republican %
1944	13.9	13.0
1948	14.8	15.2
1952	14.1	15.5
1956	16.1	15.3
1960	16.2	17.1
1964	16.8	18.1
1968	17.6	19.3
1972	19.5	17.6
1976	16.4	19.1
1980	15.8	20.1
1984	18.7	19.6

Looking at how the individual states have voted in elections since 1944 one can see that Michael Dukakis has as formidable a problem here as in the Midwest:

	1944–64		1968–84	
	Dem	Rep	Dem	Rep
Alaska (a)	1	1	0	5
Arizona	2	4	0	5
California	3	3	0	5
Colorado	2	4	0	5
Hawaii (a)	2	0	3	2
Idaho	3	3	0	5
Montana	3	3	0	5
Nevada	4	2	0	5
New Mexico	4	2	0	5
Oregon	2	4	0	5
Utah	2	4	0	5
Washington	3	3	1	4
Wyoming	2	4	0	5

Note: (a) First voted in presidential elections in 1960

The Republicans have won all five elections since 1968 in eleven out of the region's thirteen states. The Republican candidates in four out of those five elections have come from California but even the most optimistic Democratic strategist would not claim that this fact alone accounts for such a voting record. Since 1968 the Democrats have only performed well in Hawaii and succeeded in carrying Washington only once. By contrast, between 1944 and 1964 they won two-thirds of the elections in Nevada and New Mexico and half of them in California, Idaho, Montana and Washington.

Following the mid-term elections in 1986, the region's party representation was as follows:

	Democrat	Republican
Senate	10	16
House	45	40
Governors	9	4

This distribution represents a very different picture from the barren political soil for the Democrats in presidential elections. However, they have not been able to translate these state-wide votes into presidential votes in the past and will face considerable difficulties in doing so this year.

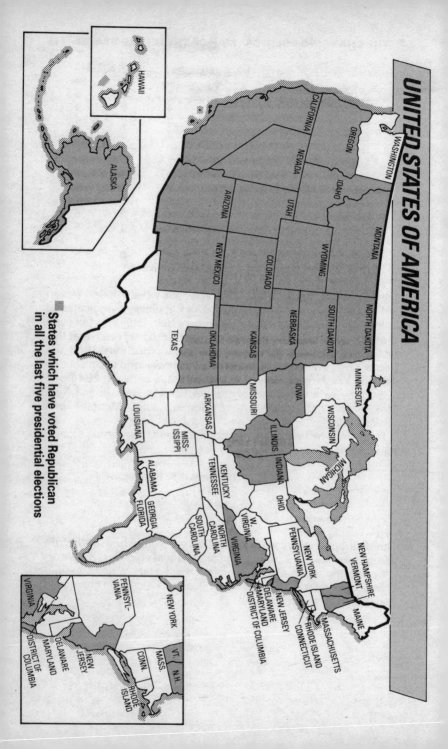

UNITED STATES OF AMERICA

States which have voted Republican in all the last five presidential elections

CHAPTER SEVEN
Profile of the Fifty States

Presidential elections have been described as not one nationwide contest but rather 50 individual state contests. This is because presidents are elected by securing a majority of electoral college votes, rather than a majority of the popular vote (although, in practice, the two have seldom been different). Chapter Three sets out the workings of the Electoral College in more detail. In this chapter we profile each of the 50 states in the Union, plus the District of Columbia.

One of the threads running through the chapter is an assessment of how the states may vote in November and how many electoral college votes they will bring to the candidate they choose. It is easy for some Americans, let alone we British, to misunderstand the nature of the Electoral College. We could look at the map in Chapter Three showing each state's electoral college votes and assume that it is a great jigsaw puzzle made up of fifty interchangeable pieces: that presidential elections are simply won by gathering the 270 electoral college votes needed from *any* combination of those 50 states. But, as John Brennan, ABC News Polling Associate, wrote in July:

> That's not how the electoral college behaves. The electoral college map is not a jigsaw puzzle with states that can be interchanged at will, pulled this way and that by circumstances or political manoeuvering and assembled and reassembled in a multitude of models that could bring an electoral majority. It is not possible for Democratic strategists to say, for example, that they'll give up New York and concentrate instead on two other smaller states whose electoral votes equal New York's. The nation just doesn't vote that way.

He went on to point out that there was an important 'organic quality' about the way individual states vote in presidential elections. Each one of the 50 states making up the Electoral College is influenced by its own past history of voting, its own political culture. It will also be influenced by developments in its own region just as much, if not more so, as by what is happening in the nation as a whole. John Brennan concluded: 'Strategy and prevailing circumstances can change that to a certain degree, but they can't undo the state's voting tradition altogether.'

With this advice in mind, the key states to watch in November are **California, Illinois, Michigan, North Carolina, Ohio** and **Texas**. Other states are important, but if these six swing to one candidate or another then we will know how the nation is voting.

ALABAMA

Population:	4,000,000
Electoral college votes:	9
1984 election result:	Reagan 61%
	Mondale 38%

Alabama, in the Deep South, has been in economic decline during the 1980s. In the 1960s and 1970s it was one of the most heavily industrialized states in the South but decline in world demand for products such as steel produced recession and relatively high unemployment.

Politically, too, the state has changed. For nearly a quarter of a century from 1962 to 1986 Alabama politics were dominated by the segregationist governor, George Wallace. He led the fight against civil rights, running as a States Rights candidate in the 1968 presidential election. Ironically in his later years he became more liberal, accepted the reality of desegregation and was voted for by a large proportion of the black electorate. Politics no longer split along strictly racial lines and moderate politicians are winning state-wide office.

Alabama's most prominent politician now is Senator Howell Heflin, a moderate southern Democrat who has proved to be a key swing vote on the Senate Judiciary Committee. He was the most important block to President Reagan's nomination of Robert Bork for the Supreme Court.

The most important political division is now economic. Poorer areas, both black and white, vote Democrat and the growing suburban areas vote Republican. Neither party predominates.

ALASKA

Population:	500,000
Electoral college votes:	3
1984 election result:	Reagan 67%
	Mondale 30%

Alaska is in every sense a state apart. Separated from the 48 continental states, it is the last outpost of the frontier spirit. If superimposed on the rest of the United States it would stretch from Florida to Canada, and from Maine to California. The state has enormous natural resources and a tiny population. That means that almost all its taxes are paid by the oil companies and personal taxation is the lowest in the Union. The citizens believe in minimal governmental interference in their lives and oppose the environmental lobby in the rest of America which they feel stops them exploiting what is rightfully theirs.

This libertarian frontier spirit has made Alaska one of the most solidly Republican states in presidential races. But with only 3 electoral college votes and vast distances to travel it would not be fiercely contested in any case.

ARIZONA

Population:	3,100,000
Electoral college votes:	7
1984 election result:	Reagan 66%
	Mondale 33%

If any state can be said to be safely Republican in presidential races then it is Arizona. The state has voted Republican in every election since 1948. Its electorate seems to share the philosophy of its most famous son, Senator Barry Goldwater – opposed to big government, against the New Deal and vehemently anti-communist. When Goldwater ran for the presidency in 1964 he was overwhelmingly defeated by President Johnson. The politics that made him so popular in Arizona (where he did win) made him suspect in the rest of the country.

This year Arizonan politics were enlivened by the impeachment of Republican Governor Evan Mecham. He thinks President Reagan is running a 'socialist superstate' and has defended the use of the word 'piccaninny' to describe black children. Mr Mecham's views enraged a wide range of political opinion. In April the state Senate stripped him of office, finding him guilty of the obstruction of justice and the misuse of state funds. He had interfered with the investigation of a death threat made by one of his staff and had lent $80,000 of public money to his family's car dealership. Mr Mecham became only the seventeenth governor in American history to be impeached.

ARKANSAS

Population:	2,400,000
Electoral college votes:	6
1984 election result:	Reagan 60%
	Mondale 38%

In 1957 Arkansas became the centre of world attention when Governor Orval Faubus tried to prevent the racial desegregation of a school in Little Rock. President Eisenhower reluctantly had to send in federal troops to uphold the Constitution. But in 1966 Arkansas elected Winthrop Rockefeller, brother of Nelson, as governor. He was one of the first southern governors to endorse integration. The state came to accept his progressive approach.

Although it is still poorer than most, the state has closed the gap considerably over the last twenty years and seems to have a bright economic future as part of the Sun Belt. Today only 5% of the population works in agriculture compared with 33% in 1950. Industry has been attracted here by the state's central location, natural resources and a population eager for work.

Democrats hold most state offices and Arkansas is probably the southern state most likely to go Democrat in presidential races. Any Democrat who cannot win here will find it difficult to take the White House.

CALIFORNIA

Population:	26,000,000
Electoral college votes:	47
1984 election result:	Reagan 58%
	Mondale 41%

If California was an independent nation it would rank as one of the wealthiest ten in the world. Its booming economy is underpinned by high-technology industry and a plentiful supply of relatively cheap immigrant labour.

The last four Republican presidents have either come from California or gone to live there in retirement. In presidential elections it appears to have become a Republican state. In the close contests of 1960, 1968 and 1976 the voters backed the Republican candidate by small margins on each occasion. This time Michael Dukakis has been doing well in state polls and has realistic hopes of carrying California in November.

Certainly some state elections have boosted the Democrats' hopes. Two years ago many commentators were surprised by the re-election of Democratic Senator Alan Cranston. A liberal supporter of disarmament and high government spending he was challenged by a popular Republican, Ed Zschau (pronounced like shout without the t). Zschau's politics seemed to reflect the mood of California in the 1980s. He was tough on foreign policy, an enthusiastic supporter of market economics and tolerant on social and cultural issues. President Reagan came and campaigned for the Republicans but despite that the then 72-year-old Cranston held on to his Senate seat.

On the same day, however, the electorate enthusiastically returned Republican Governor George Deukmejian with a larger percentage of the vote than Ronald Reagan has ever received in California. Deukmejian, whom supporters call 'The real Duke', is more Reaganite than the President himself. He has been tipped as a future presidential candidate.

Personality clearly plays an important part in determining close contests. California's electorate is getting plenty of opportunities to study both candidates. With more electoral college votes than any other state, both Bush and Dukakis are spending more time, money and energy here than anywhere else.

COLORADO

Population:	3,100,000
Electoral college votes:	8
1984 election result:	Reagan 63%
	Mondale 35%

Colorado has in recent years produced a number of liberal Democrats who have achieved national prominence. Most notable among them was Gary Hart who was a senator here until 1986. Still in Congress is Representative Pat Schroeder from Denver. She coined the phrase 'Teflon President' about Ronald Reagan because scandal did not stick to him. Schroeder considered running for president herself this time but in a tearful statement announced she would not enter the race, mainly because of the complete invasion of privacy it inevitably entails.

Despite the fact that its most prominent politicians have been liberals, the state tends towards the Republicans in presidential contests. It was the only western state to reject Franklin Roosevelt twice and strongly supported Richard Nixon in the close 1960 election. Last time round Ronald Reagan picked up almost two-thirds of the vote.

CONNECTICUT

Population:	3,300,000
Electoral college votes:	8
1984 election result:	Reagan 61%
	Mondale 39%

Connecticut has had Democratic governors for 26 of the last 30 years, the main state offices are held by Democrats, and although its Senate representation is evenly split, the Republican Senator Lowell Weicker is fiercely independent and has made no secret of his opposition to the Reagan administration on a wide range of disparate issues.

But the Democrats' position in the state is not as solid as this might suggest. Connecticut voters have backed the Republicans in the last four presidential elections and the Reagan defence policy has been popular in a state with a large defence industry. George Bush grew up here and his father Prescott Bush represented the state in the Senate. If he wins nationally in November, Connecticut will probably be in his column.

DELAWARE

Population:	700,000
Electoral college votes:	3
1984 election result:	Reagan 60%
	Mondale 40%

Delaware is small. It is the second-smallest state in the Union and has the third-smallest population. Nevertheless it is prosperous. Its wealth is built on liberal incorporation laws that encourage large companies to register their existence here. Delaware is, technically at least, the home of many of America's biggest corporations.

With just 3 electoral college votes it does not usually play much of a role in presidential elections. The entire state can be reached by television stations in neighbouring Pennsylvania, so presidential campaigns do not invest much time or money here.

However, this year the state did produce a candidate for the nominations of both the major parties. Liberal Democratic Senator Joe Biden was running hard until an 'attack video' issued by an aide to Michael Dukakis showed that Biden had plagiarized a speech by Neil Kinnock. He was forced to withdraw. Former Governor Pierre du Pont tried to win the Republican nomination. But the early primary voters were not attracted by his brand of *laissez-faire* liberalism nor his patrician reputation.

DISTRICT OF COLUMBIA

Population:	700,000
Electoral college votes:	3
1984 election result:	Reagan 14%
	Mondale 85%

The Founding Fathers worried that the population of the capital would try to exert influence on the legislature and decided therefore to give authority over the District of Columbia to Congress. Only in the last 25 years has the district received an element of self-rule.

In 1964 DC was given 3 electoral college votes. In every election, including the 1984 Reagan landslide, it has voted Democrat. The District of Columbia is in fact not only more Democratic than any state but more heavily Democratic than any county anywhere in the country. Two-thirds of the population is black and nearly one-fifth has an income below the poverty level. No one expects DC to do anything but vote heavily for Michael Dukakis on 8 November.

FLORIDA

Population:	11,200,000
Electoral college votes:	21
1984 election result:	Reagan 65%
	Mondale 35%

Florida has boomed since the war. It used to be a backward state relying on agriculture and tourism, but successive waves of northerners flying down to live in the sun have transformed Florida beyond recognition. In the last ten years the population has risen by more than 30%. It is now the fifth most populous state and has the second-fastest economic growth rate. Around 900 people a day settle here.

Northern Republican Yankees were the first to arrive in the late 1940s, followed by ethnic blue-collar Democrats also fleeing the Frost Belt. Immigrants from Cuba and Central America have added to the ethnic mix. Mostly conservative, they have helped the Republicans.

The present governor, Bob Martinez, is Florida's first Hispanic governor. A disillusioned Democrat, he defected to the Republicans and captured the governorship two years ago. It is only the second time the Republicans have won it this century.

Both presidential candidates will be competing hard for Florida's 21 electoral college votes. The state voted heavily for Reagan in 1984 but Democrats do win state-wide office here and the state was in Jimmy Carter's column in 1976.

GEORGIA

Population:	5,700,000
Electoral college votes:	12
1984 election result:	Reagan 60%
	Mondale 40%

In the days of the solid Democratic South, Georgia was as solid as anywhere. In 1960 it gave John F. Kennedy a higher percentage of the presidential poll than even his native Massachusetts. But in the wake of the Kennedy–Johnson civil rights legislation the state's white voters turned against the Democrats. They supported Barry Goldwater in 1964, when nationally he was swamped by the Johnson landslide, and in 1968 backed the States Rights candidate George Wallace.

The election of Governor Jimmy Carter in 1970 marked a significant change in Georgian political life. He made it clear that the days of racial segregation were over and became one of the leading politicians of the new integrated South.

In state elections the Democrats still dominate. They hold every state-wide office and have massive majorities in the state legislature. One of their senators, Sam Nunn, chairman of the Senate Armed Services Committee, is a major force in Washington and was considered for the vice-presidential nomination until he said he did not want it because he valued his independence too much. If Michael Dukakis is to win in November he will need to win in states like Georgia.

HAWAII

Population: 1,100,000
Electoral college votes: 4
1984 election result: Reagan 55%
                              Mondale 44%

America's newest state is made up of a group of islands in the Pacific. Since the Pearl Harbor naval base was built after the First World War, Hawaii has been a vitally important centre for the American military in the region. More than 50,000 personnel are based here and the military installations are one of the biggest local employers. Hawaii goes heavily Democratic in state elections and leans towards the Democrats in presidential contests. Four years ago, though losing, Walter Mondale had one of his best results here and in 1980 it was one of only six states Jimmy Carter won.

Senior Senator Daniel Inouye has a considerable national reputation. He gave the keynote speech at the troubled 1968 Democratic convention in Chicago and was recently praised by commentators for his tough questioning of witnesses during the Senate's Iran–Contra hearings.

IDAHO

Population:	1,000,000
Electoral college votes:	4
1984 election result:	Reagan 72%
	Mondale 26%

Idaho is one of America's fastest expanding states: its population has grown by more than 50% in the last twenty years. The changing demography has produced a shift from the Democrats to the Republicans. It is now one of the most conservative states with an antipathy to big government. Good Democratic candidates do win state office, and the current governor, Cecil Andrus, is a Democrat, but in presidential elections the Republicans assume that it will fall in safely behind their candidate.

ILLINOIS

Population:	11,700,000
Electoral college votes:	24
1984 election result:	Reagan 56%
	Mondale 43%

Illinois is a crucial state to win. It has backed the victor in all but one presidential election in the past 70 years and with 24 electoral college votes it is always vigorously contested. Politics here are competitive. The governorship is in Republican hands, but both the Senate seats are held by Democrats. There are relatively small Democratic majorities in both houses of the state legislature.

Since the New Deal, Chicago, the state's main city, has been predominantly Democratic. Its politics were dominated for most of the century by the Democratic machine. The height of 'boss' politics here was in the 1950s and 1960s when Richard Daley was mayor. The city's payrolls were full of patronage appointments right down to the lowest level. In return for jobs and contracts the machine demanded electoral support. Where that was not forthcoming the Republicans claim they simply rigged the counts. John F. Kennedy, who won Illinois by a narrow margin in 1960, was never himself convinced that the Daley machine had not fixed the Cook County count. But the machine collapsed in the 1970s and Chicago politics are now a great deal cleaner than they once were.

In the Chicago suburbs and the rural parts of the state there are enough Republican voters to elect state office holders. The present governor, James Thompson, has gained a national reputation as a leading figure on the liberal wing of the Republican Party.

The other politician who has made a significant mark on national politics is the liberal Democratic Senator Paul Simon. This year he was, at 59, the oldest Democrat to compete for the presidential nomination. He had limited electoral success but his practice of always wearing a bow tie made him, in the early days of the campaign, the most easily recognizable candidate in a large field.

INDIANA

Population:	5,600,000
Electoral college votes:	12
1984 election result:	Reagan 62%
	Mondale 38%

Indiana is a predominantly Republican state. In presidential elections it has only backed the Democrats in landslide years and nothing suggests the situation will be different this November. The state remains the home of old-style patronage-based machine politics. The Republican machine is dominant. The Republicans have provided the governors since 1968, fill most of the state-wide offices, have majorities in both houses of the state legislature and send two senators to Washington.

The senior senator is Richard Lugar who is up for re-election this year. As chairman of the Senate Foreign Relations Committee he has played a major part in shaping foreign policy. He has generally supported the administration but has led the way on certain issues; for instance encouraging the White House to remove its support from Ferdinand Marcos in the Philippines and back Cory Aquino.

The junior senator is Dan Quayle, George Bush's surprise choice as his vice-presidential running mate.

IOWA

Population:	3,000,000
Electoral college votes:	8
1984 election result:	Reagan 53%
	Mondale 46%

The state's role in presidential elections is quite out of proportion to its size. By holding the first caucuses at the beginning of election year when the snow is still thick on the ground, Iowa plays a significant part in thinning out the field of prospective candidates and picking out rising stars to watch. This time round Republican voters gave George Bush a nasty early shock by backing Bob Dole. The Vice-President had to work hard on his image to put the damage right in time for New Hampshire.

The electorate is culturally conservative but liberal on foreign policy. The most agricultural state in the Union, it prospers by exporting food abroad, in particular wheat to the Soviet Union. Candidates who have supported grain embargoes of the USSR have not been popular here. This year Iowa, like other corn-belt states, has been hit hard by the drought. Michael Dukakis visited the state at the end of June to show his concern for the drought-stricken farmers and their families. Whether the drought will have any impact on voting behaviour in November is unclear. But the Bush message that ordinary people are economically better off under the Reagan administration may look unconvincing in parts of Iowa.

Although the state has leaned towards the Republicans in recent years, if it is a close race nationally it could go either way.

KANSAS

Population:	2,500,000
Electoral college votes:	7
1984 election result:	Reagan 66%
	Mondale 33%

Kansas lies at the exact geographical centre of the continental United States. In every sense this is middle America. It is farm country and solidly Republican. Kansas voters have not sent a Democrat to the Senate since 1932. Kansas produced Alf Landon, the Republican who bravely but hopelessly stood against Roosevelt at the height of the New Deal. His daughter Nancy

Kassebaum represents the state in the Senate today.

The senior senator is the Republican's Senate leader, Bob Dole. When running for the presidential nomination this year he made much of his small-town roots in Russell, Kansas. His moderate brand of politics is that of the Kansas Republicans: trust in the free market but also a belief that the government has a role to play in helping the less fortunate.

KENTUCKY

Population:	3,600,000
Electoral college votes:	9
1984 election result:	Reagan 60%
	Mondale 38%

Kentucky is a largely rural state, famous for its thoroughbred horses and tobacco. Politics here still reflect the divisions of the Civil War. Kentucky was split on the question of slavery. Those parts of the state that were pro-Union still lean towards the Republicans. Those who backed the Confederacy tend to support the Democrats.

In state elections the electorate is still predominantly Democratic. In presidential races they have shown a willingness to back Democrats like Jimmy Carter towards whom they feel political sympathy but have not been willing to support old-fashioned northern liberals like Humphrey, McGovern or Mondale. As in much of the South, Dukakis will have to hope his candidacy is viewed more sympathetically than those of recent northern Democrats.

LOUISIANA

Population:	4,500,000
Electoral college votes:	10
1984 election result:	Reagan 61%
	Mondale 38%

Louisiana in the Deep South is a swampy state where the temperature and humidity in mid-summer can make life without air conditioning very uncomfortable. In recent years its economy was helped by oil in the Gulf of Mexico but a drop in the world price has hit the state hard and it has been slipping back down the economic league table.

The most famous politician in the state's history was Huey Long. A populist governor, then senator, first elected in 1928, he invested in the state's infrastructure and introduced social welfare programmes before the New Deal. FDR thought Long would be his most serious opponent for the 1936 Democratic presidential nomination, but Long was murdered in 1935. However for decades afterwards state politics split along pro- and anti-Long lines, with many protégés and relations serving in public office.

Democrats still fill all the state offices but in national elections the electorate has tended to back Republican candidates. Nevertheless with the recent decline in the state's economic fortunes the Democrats will hope to do better this November.

MAINE

Population:	1,100,000
Electoral college votes:	4
1984 election result:	Reagan 61%
	Mondale 39%

There is a saying about Maine's electoral behaviour, 'as goes Maine, so goes the nation'. Its origin seems to have been more that its state elections were in September rather than November, than that it was in any sense a good litmus test for the national result. Certainly in close elections since the war it has been a very bad predictor. It is the only state to have backed the loser in all four of the recent close presidential races. It voted for Dewey when Truman won in 1948, Nixon when Kennedy won in 1960, Humphrey when Nixon won in 1968 and Ford when Carter won in 1976.

Another oddity is that Maine is the only state that does not insist its electoral votes must all go to one candidate. Two of them are awarded on the state-wide result while the other two are awarded on the basis of the results in each of the congressional districts. With just two congressional districts this has little practical effect, but some have suggested that other larger states should adopt the same practice.

This time round the Republicans will be claiming their candidate is a local: George Bush has a holiday home at Kennebunkport.

MARYLAND

Population:	4,400,000
Electoral college votes:	10
1984 election result:	Reagan 53%
	Mondale 47%

Michael Dukakis's campaign will be encouraged by the recent trend in Maryland's voting behaviour. It was once regularly a closely contested state in presidential elections and a good predictor of the national outcome. But in recent years it has become more and more Democratic. It was one of only six states to support President Carter in 1980 and four years ago it gave Walter Mondale his fifth-best result.

The change in voting behaviour is explained by a significant influx of black voters who previously lived in the neighbouring District of Columbia. Maryland now has the nation's largest concentration of middle-class suburban blacks, most of whom have stuck with their Democratic roots.

The Democrats hold the governorship, both Senate seats, large majorities in the state legislature and send six congressmen to Washington as opposed to the Republicans' two.

MASSACHUSETTS

Population:	6,000,000
Electoral college votes:	13
1984 election result:	Reagan 51%
	Mondale 48%

Massachusetts is one of the most Democratic states. Four years ago it only just supported President Reagan when he was sweeping the board almost everywhere else. This time with the popular Governor Michael Dukakis as the Democratic candidate there can be little doubt which way the Bay state will vote, though George Bush supporters will continue to remind voters that their man was born here too.

Since Dukakis was returned to the governorship for the second time in 1982 the state has experienced an economic boom based on high-technology industry. Dukakis has taken the credit for the 'Massachusetts Miracle'. His opponents say it would have happened without him and some argue that the Reagan defence programme has done more for Massachusetts' economic upturn than anything else.

Another almost-certain winner in Massachusetts this year will be Edward Kennedy, whose Senate seat is up for election. The brother of the late President is the state's most influential politician in Washington. Kennedy seems to have given up his presidential aspirations and instead appears happy with his position as a leading senator and best-known proponent of increased government spending on welfare programmes.

MICHIGAN

Population:	9,300,00
Electoral college votes:	20
1984 election result:	Reagan 59%
	Mondale 40%

The development of the mass-produced motor car transformed Michigan in the first 30 years of the century from a quiet, mainly agricultural state into a booming industrial one. A number of the pioneers of mass production, including Henry Ford, based their factories here. The population of Detroit increased fivefold between 1900 and 1930. For decades the industry provided the state's economic backbone. In the late 1970s Chrysler, Ford and General Motors all had major problems and were forced to cut back on their labour forces. In the mid-1980s an economic upturn began, not based on the performance of the big three but rather on new and more diverse businesses.

The state has also changed politically. In the 1960s it was safely Democratic, but it voted for Gerald Ford in 1976 (he comes from Michigan) and enthusiastically backed Ronald Reagan in 1980 and 1984. But in state-wide elections the Democrats have been doing well. Governor Jim Blanchard, who two years ago retained the office by beating the first-ever black Republican gubernatorial candidate, has been credited for much of Michigan's recent success. Michael Dukakis will hope to benefit from the local party's reputation in November.

MINNESOTA

Population:	4,200,000
Electoral college votes:	10
1984 election result:	Reagan 50%
	Mondale 50%

When southern Democrats look for examples of northern liberals their electorates do not like as presidential candidates, the names of Hubert Humphrey and Walter Mondale are normally mentioned. Both of these distinguished liberal presidential candidates were at one time senators from Minnesota and grew up in the tradition of the Democratic-Farmer-Labor Party (DFL).

The DFL for a long time dominated politics here and Minnesota has traditionally been solidly Democratic. But that is no longer the case. Walter Mondale won his home state by less than 4,000 votes in 1984 and the Republicans now hold both Senate seats. In this election, with no Minnesotan on the Democratic national ticket, the state could go Republican.

MISSISSIPPI

Population:	2,700,000
Electoral college votes:	7
1984 election result:	Reagan 62%
	Mondale 37%

In the days before Civil Rights there was no state that enforced segregation more firmly than Mississippi. When Congress began to pass civil rights legislation, the white electorate here did what it could to resist. In 1964 Goldwater got 87% of the vote and even in 1968, after many blacks had started to vote, George Wallace, the States Rights candidate, picked up 63%.

In the 1970s, however, integration did take hold and the state benefited economically as a result. More talented black people stayed and worked in the state, rather than fleeing to the more liberal north, and industry and commerce from out of state became more inclined to invest in Mississippi.

The Republicans did for a time benefit from the racial polarization, but there are now signs that that polarization is breaking down and Mississippi party politics may be entering a competitive period.

MISSOURI

Population:	5,100,000
Electoral college votes:	11
1984 election result:	Reagan 60%
	Mondale 40%

Missouri was President Harry Truman's home state. Through the 1950s and 1960s it was strongly inclined to the Democrats, but in recent years there has been a distinct shift towards the Republicans. The Democrats have a majority in both houses of the state legislature and a 5 to 4 advantage in congressmen but the Republicans hold both Senate seats. In fact of the nine state-wide elected offices only one is filled by a Democrat.

On past form Missouri is a good indicator of the national result. Only once in the past century has its electorate backed a losing presidential candidate. That was in 1956 when they voted for Adlai Stevenson rather than Dwight Eisenhower. Last time round President Reagan got almost his precise national percentage here.

The state's best-known contemporary politician is Richard Gephardt, who represents the 3rd Congressional District. He won this year's Democratic caucus in Iowa and for a time was Dukakis's main opponent for the nomination.

MONTANA

Population:	900,000
Electoral college votes:	4
1984 election result:	Reagan 60%
	Mondale 38%

Car registration plates in Montana proudly boast that this is the 'Big Sky State' and it is easy to see why. Driving across Montana in summer the sky really does seem to stretch further and higher than elsewhere. The state's beautiful open scenery attracts tourists from both coasts, either crossing the country from the East, or West Coast residents heading through Oregon, Idaho and Montana on the way down to Yellowstone. In size it is America's fourth-largest state. In population it is the seventh-smallest.

In Senate elections the Democrats normally come out on top. They have won every Senate seat in the state's history bar one: the contest in 1946. But the Republicans do win other elections here. One of Montana's two congressmen is a Republican and the parties have almost equal representation in the state legislature. In presidential races Montana is a swing state but with just 4 electoral college votes and huge distances to cover candidates rarely campaign here.

NEBRASKA

Population:	1,700,000
Electoral college votes:	5
1984 election result:	Reagan 71%
	Mondale 29%

The chat-show host Johnny Carson is popular throughout middle America as the embodiment of all-American values. Nowhere is that more true than here in Nebraska, his home state. The main street in his home town of Norfolk is called Johnny Carson Boulevard. Nebraskans believe in God, family, the flag and Republican presidents.

A Republican candidate could in fact be forgiven for taking Nebraska for granted. In 1980 it was Governor Reagan's second-best state, in 1984 it was President Reagan's fourth best. In all the recent close races – 1960, 1968 and 1976 it stayed with the Republicans.

Despite being conservative, Nebraska became the first state two years ago to have two women as the major party candidates for governor. The winner, predictably, was Kay Orr, a Republican and enthusiastic Reagan loyalist.

NEVADA

Population:	1,000,000
Electoral college votes:	4
1984 election result:	Reagan 66%
	Mondale 32%

Nevada is built on gambling. Since it was legalized in the 1930s, Reno and Las Vegas have boomed. The population has grown from under 100,000 to 1 million. The casinos and hotels that go with them are now one of the state's two major employers. The other is the federal government's nuclear testing programme. Ninety per cent of the land, which is mostly desert, is owned by the government and a large proportion of America's military nuclear testing takes place here.

Nevada used to swing with the national political trend. It backed Kennedy over Nixon in 1960 and Nixon over Humphrey in 1968. More recently its new residents, many of them here to make a quick buck, have moved the state heavily behind the Republican Party.

NEW HAMPSHIRE

Population:	1,100,000
Electoral college votes:	4
1984 election result:	Reagan 69%
	Mondale 31%

Despite its tiny population New Hampshire plays a major role in presidential elections by holding the first primary of the electoral season. State law says that it must be a week before any other state's. It is not clear what would happen if another state passed similar legislation. Since 1952, when the modern-style primary was established, no one has won the presidency without first winning their party's primary here. The record will not be broken this year; both Michael Dukakis and George Bush won their respective primaries. For Mr Bush it was a crucial victory, coming as it did just days after defeat by Bob Dole in the Iowa caucuses.

In presidential elections New Hampshire is one of the nation's most Republican states. But Dukakis will be hoping that his vocal opposition to the construction of the Seabrook nuclear power station will help him here. Most of the electorate is strongly opposed to it and this strictly local issue might swing some votes this November.

NEW JERSEY

Population:	7,500,000
Electoral college votes:	16
1984 election result:	Reagan 60%
	Mondale 39%

New Jersey is a bustling East Coast industrial state. In the 1980s a massive expansion of high-technology industry has produced a growth rate that is higher than its regional competitors, Massachusetts and New York.

Two politicians dominate the political scene. Democratic Senator Bill Bradley, a former basketball star and Rhodes Scholar, is admired in Washington as an independent-minded and skilful legislator. He was tipped as a presidential candidate himself but decided not to seek the nomination.

Governor Thomas Kean (pronounced kane) is a leading liberal Republican. He is known for his desire to bring women and minorities into the Republican Party mainstream. It was because of this that Vice-President Bush chose him to deliver the keynote speech at the convention in New Orleans. In a recent book, *The Politics of Inclusion*, Kean set out ways to reach beyond the Republicans' traditional wealthy, white-collar base. One of New Jersey's most popular governors, Kean was resoundingly re-elected in 1985 with an unprecedented 60% of the black vote. Four years earlier, he had edged into the governor's office by the smallest-ever margin.

In presidential politics New Jersey has normally leaned towards the Republicans. In the close race of 1960 it did back Kennedy, but in the other close contests of 1968 and 1976 it was in the Republican column.

NEW MEXICO

Population: 1,600,000
Electoral college votes: 5
1984 election result: Reagan 60%
                 Mondale 39%

New Mexico is a meeting point of cultures. Nearly a third of the population speak Spanish as their first language. Most are not new immigrants from south of the border but rather descendants of Spanish settlers or much earlier Mexican immigrants. Hispanic–Indian culture is predominant in much of the state, especially in the north and west.

Politics here used to be 'boss' dominated, with the large Hispanic vote controlled on a corrupt patronage basis. Offices and the spoils of office were divided in smoke-filled rooms between 'Anglos' and 'Hispanics'.

Nowadays politics is cleaner. There is little evidence of ethnic block voting. In presidential races New Mexico has in the past been a very good predictor of the national result. Since statehood it has backed only one loser: Gerald Ford in 1976.

NEW YORK

Population:	19,000,000
Electoral college votes:	36
1984 election result:	Reagan 54%
	Mondale 46%

Over the decades, New York has produced many of the nation's leading politicians: Roosevelt, Dewey, Eisenhower (resident here when he won the presidency in 1952) and Rockefeller to name but a few. Today its politics are still watched by the rest of the nation with a mixture of fascination and disdain.

The heyday of machine politics is long since gone but the state's politicians are as colourful as ever. The two dominant figures of the 1980s are Governor Mario Cuomo and New York City Mayor Ed Koch. They have long been rivals within the Democratic Party. Koch beat Cuomo for the job of mayor in 1977, Cuomo beat Koch for the governorship in 1982. The two men differ on issues – Cuomo is more liberal than the Mayor. They differ, too, in their approach: Cuomo excels as a passionate advocate and an accomplished orator; Koch prefers sarcastic wit.

The Governor was expected to run for the Democratic nomination this year. Had he done so Michael Dukakis's road to Atlanta might have been very different. But Cuomo's decision not to run has not dampened speculation that he will one day seek the nomination.

New York is often thought of as a very liberal, pro-Democratic state. In truth it is only marginally more Democratic than the national average. The Democrats in the City are more or less balanced by Republicans in upstate New York. The state's reputation as being very liberal probably comes from a casual observation of its Democratic primary where there is indeed a distinctive left-wing vote.

Michael Dukakis will be expecting to do well here but the Democrats will not take the state for granted. There has been a significant population shift from the City to the suburbs in the 1980s and this has favoured the Republicans.

NORTH CAROLINA

Population:	6,100,000
Electoral college votes:	13
1984 election result:	Reagan 62%
	Mondale 38%

North Carolina is unenthusiastic about northern Democrats. It has been prepared to consider southern Democratic presidential candidates but this year the Bush campaign is confident the electorate will back the Vice-President.

State races, however, are competitive. Four years ago North Carolina saw the most expensive Senate race in America's history. It pitted the state's Democratic Governor Jim Hunt against the arch-conservative Republican Senator Jesse Helms. Hunt stood for government help to encourage economic growth, the abolition of all vestiges of racial segregation and policies aimed at bringing the state fully into the American mainstream. Helms by contrast advocated fiercely conservative policies. He believes in an unbridled free market and the values of fundamental Christianity. Helms won the election by a narrow margin and remained in place as one of the most conservative politicians in Washington.

Other North Carolinan office-holders, however, are more moderate. Governor James Martin, a Republican, has implemented policies similar to those of his Democratic predecessor, Jim Hunt, including increased public spending on education. The state's junior senator is Terry Sanford, a former governor. Many thought the electorate would consider him too liberal but he surprised commentators by winning in 1986, despite spending a million dollars less than his Republican opponent.

NORTH DAKOTA

Population:	700,000
Electoral college votes:	3
1984 election result:	Reagan 65%
	Mondale 34%

North Dakota is not a place of rapid change. One in four of the population still lives on farms. That is the largest proportion in any state and has changed little in the past 50 years. Historically the electorate has backed the Republicans. In 1980 this inclination was reinforced by anger at President Carter's grain embargo against the Soviet Union. He was beaten 64% to 26% by Ronald Reagan. In 1984 Reagan again carried the state very easily.

The Democrats must look to other results for encouragement. They won the governorship four years ago and in 1986 Kent Conrad won a Senate seat from Republican Mark Andrews. The state's other senator and congressman are also both Democrats.

OHIO

Population:	11,000,000
Electoral college votes:	23
1984 election result:	Reagan 59%
	Mondale 40%

Ohio is a key state to win. With 23 electoral college votes it is being contested as keenly as ever this year. The industrial north-east of the state is heavily Democratic. Governor Richard Celeste, who has expressed presidential ambitions himself, got 70% of the vote there in 1986. The rest of Ohio leans towards the Republicans.

The state's best-known politician is undoubtedly Democratic Senator John Glenn, the first American to orbit the earth. He can only smile when Jake Garn of Utah is described as the first senator in space. An advocate of middle-American values, Glenn is always safely returned. Michael Dukakis has worked hard for his enthastic backing, only too aware of Ohio's vital importance in any winning strategy. A fortnight before Atlanta Dukakis encouraged speculation that Glenn would be his running mate. When addressing a rally in Ohio he elicited enthusiastic support for the Senator by asking a partisan crowd who they wanted on the ticket.

The Republicans are pursuing Ohio's voters with equal gusto. It has been said in the past that the Republicans cannot win without carrying Ohio. President Reagan's result here in 1984 was similar to his national average but Vice-President Bush cannot be encouraged by the knowledge that there is not a single Republican holding state-wide office.

OKLAHOMA

Population: 3,300,000
Electoral college votes: 8
1984 election result: Reagan 69%
                                Mondale 31%

Oklahoma politics have historically been split along geographical lines. The south of the state, settled from Texas, Arkansas and other parts of the South, voted Democrat. The north, settled from Kansas, backed the Republican Party. Politics here are competitive but the Republicans have something of an advantage because of their strength in the big population centres of Tulsa and Oklahoma City.

In the last 25 years the two oil-rich cities have both grown significantly giving the Republicans a considerable boost. The recent fall in the price of oil has shaken confidence but the Republicans still expect the electorate in both Tulsa and Oklahoma City to back the party. In 1964 the cities cast just over a third of the state's votes. Despite the fact that they both went for Barry Goldwater in 1964, Lyndon Johnson carried the state. They now account for a little more than half the vote. In a close election they are likely to tip Oklahoma to the Republicans.

Two years ago the Republicans took the governorship from the Democrats. The state sends one senator from each party to Washington but the Democrats have a majority in both houses of the state legislature.

OREGON

Population: 2,600,000
Electoral college votes: 7
1984 election result: Reagan 57%
                                Mondale 43%

Oregon in the north-west is remote. Its beautiful coastline, with massive dunes and vast forests, have made it a popular vacation destination for southern Californians prepared to make the long drive north. Local awareness of the state's beauty has made the electorate environmentally conscious. It is a foolish candidate who ignores the environmental lobby.

The state's economy rests on forestry and its position as a gateway to trade with the east. As in Washington to the north, trade protectionist policies are unpopular here.

Like other thinly populated states in the north-west, Oregon will get little attention in this campaign. But the Democrats will be hoping for success. It used to be a Republican state but in the close election of 1976 it only just backed Gerald Ford and last time round it was one of Walter Mondale's best results.

PENNSYLVANIA

Population:	12,000,000
Electoral college votes:	25
1984 election result:	Reagan 53%
	Mondale 46%

This is where the Founding Fathers met to draw up the Constitution. The state's biggest city, Philadelphia, was then the most important in the country and had reasonable expectations of remaining so. It still is a major city but has been outgrown by others. Philadelphia and Pennsylvania are no longer at the hub of the nation. However, anywhere with 25 electoral college votes will always be vigorously contested.

Pennsylvania was once Republican. It was the only large state to stick with Hoover and oppose Roosevelt in 1932. The New Deal, however, changed political allegiances. Philadelphia moved to the Democrats, making Pennsylvania a swing state. It voted Democrat in the close races of 1960, 1968 and 1976, but a recent population shift to the suburbs may be assisting the Republicans. Democrat Robert Casey was elected governor two years ago but both Senate seats are in Republican hands.

Nevertheless, Michael Dukakis has looked at Walter Mondale's relatively good 1984 result and is hoping to do well here.

RHODE ISLAND

Population:	1,000,000
Electoral college votes:	4
1984 election result:	Reagan 52%
	Mondale 48%

Neither party usually campaigns very hard for Rhode Island's 4 electoral college votes. It is one of the nation's most solidly Democratic states and only goes Republican in landslide years. Rhode Island has only sent one Republican to the Senate in nearly 60 years and between 1940 and 1978 did not elect a single Republican congressman. Both houses of the state legislature are heavily Democratic.

In 1980 Governor Reagan had his second-worst result here and four years later the state gave the President just 52%, when he was stacking up huge majorities almost everywhere else.

SOUTH CAROLINA

Population:	3,300,000
Electoral college votes:	8
1984 election result:	Reagan 64%
	Mondale 36%

South Carolina has undergone immense economic, social and political change since the war. It used to be one of the poorest states, with a considerable proportion of the population existing on subsistence agriculture, but a post-war influx of new industry and an expansion of military facilities has seen incomes grow to near the national average.

The social change has been similar to that experienced throughout the South. Civil rights legislation brought blacks within the polity and white supremacy is now dead.

The state used to be solidly Democratic. It gave Roosevelt 88% in 1944. But the situation in the late 1980s is more confused. Black voters overwhelmingly support the Democrats, wealthy whites the Republicans. The swing voters are middle-income whites. They have twice backed Ronald Reagan. Lee Atwater, a native of the state and one of Bush's senior campaign managers, will hope their allegiance will transfer to the Vice-President.

SOUTH DAKOTA

Population:	700,000
Electoral college votes:	3
1984 election result:	Reagan 63%
	Mondale 37%

Historically South Dakota has been a Republican state. In the three decades up until 1970 it had a Democrat in the governor's office for just two years. But in the early 1970s anti-Vietnam war feeling persuaded a considerable proportion of the electorate to back its native son George McGovern, a Democrat. Over a period of years his supporters won numerous state offices and McGovern himself nearly carried the state against Nixon in 1972.

In the mid-1970s there was a shift back to the Right. The Democrats will hope to benefit from problems the farmers are suffering but they will be only too aware that in both 1980 and 1984 South Dakota gave Ronald Reagan one of his best results.

TENNESSEE

Population:	4,800,000
Electoral college votes:	11
1984 election result:	Reagan 58%
	Mondale 42%

Tennessee's best-known politician today is Democratic Senator Al Gore Jnr. He was elected in 1984 after Republican Howard Baker decided not to seek re-election. Both men were talked about as possible vice-presidential candidates for their respective parties.

Senator Gore was a candidate for the Democratic presidential nomination. A Harvard-educated expert on defence and education, he did well in the southern-dominated Super Tuesday contests. But he failed to gain enough support north of the Mason-Dixon line to be a serious challenge to Michael Dukakis.

Baker served as President Reagan's chief of staff after the Iran–Contra crisis. He stepped down this June, ostensibly because of his wife's and step-mother's poor health. The resignation raised speculation that he was interested in the vice-presidency. Howard Baker did little to discourage the suggestions.

In 1980 President Carter only just lost here and in 1984 Walter Mondale got his best southern vote. In a good year for the Democrats nationally they should be able to take Tennessee.

TEXAS

Population:	16,000,000
Electoral college votes:	29
1984 election result:	Reagan 64%
	Mondale 36%

The third most populous state and the second largest, Texas is a major prize in the presidential contest. The late Lyndon Johnson's home state is politically competitive but in the 1980s has leaned towards the Republicans.

George Bush, who moved here as a young man and set up his own oil business, will want to win Texas more than anywhere. But his record in his adopted state is not good. He lost the Republican primary to Ronald Reagan in 1980, as well as the Senate races in 1964 and 1970. In 1970 his opponent was Lloyd Bentsen, this year's Democratic vice-presidential candidate.

Texas is vital to the Democrats. Since statehood every Democratic president has carried it. John F. Kennedy gave Lyndon Johnson a place on the ticket in 1960 largely because of the state's electoral college votes. In the close elections of 1968 and 1976 Texas went Democrat. The 29 electoral college votes it has this year were the main reason for inviting Bentsen to join the ticket. Eighteen years after Bentsen first beat Bush, the Dukakis strategists are hoping he will help their man do the same.

UTAH

Population:	1,700,000
Electoral college votes:	5
1984 election result:	Reagan 75%
	Mondale 25%

Utah is the world centre of the Mormon religion. The Church of Latter Day Saints has an enormous influence over everyday life here. It takes conservative positions on all political and social issues. The electorate does likewise. The capital Salt Lake City is probably the cleanest state capital in America. Litter-bugs are unpopular here. The population is God-fearing and is conscious of civic responsibility. It is also Republican.

Utah's best-known politician is Republican Senator Jake Garn, who went into space on the shuttle Discovery. Chairman of the Senate Space Committee, he is NASA's most important ally in Washington.

The state has been the most Republican in the nation in the last three presidential elections. It sends no Democrats to Washington and elects none to state-wide office.

VERMONT

Population:	500,000
Electoral college votes:	3
1984 election result:	Reagan 58%
	Mondale 41%

The state seal shows fields, a pine tree and a cow: there is not a person in sight. It is entirely appropriate for this beautiful, sparsely populated state. Vermont is popular as a weekend get-away for people living in Boston and other urban parts of the north-east. Its green hills and white weather-boarded houses make it an archetypal New England state. Its prosperity is based on tourism and high-technology industry. IBM is the state's biggest employer.

The state used to be solidly Republican. In 1936 it was one of only two states not to go for Franklin Roosevelt. But newcomers to the state have tended to be Democrats and it is not as Republican as it was. Vermont has only ever backed one Democratic presidential candidate; that was Lyndon Johnson in 1964. But the change in population and the proximity of Michael Dukakis's home state may help the Democrats this November.

VIRGINIA

Population:	5,600,000
Electoral college votes:	12
1984 election result:	Reagan 62%
	Mondale 37%

When the Founding Fathers met, Virginia was the richest and most populous state but now it only edges into the top fifteen. In presidential contests the state is Republican. Barry Goldwater is the only Republican in recent years to have lost here.

At state level and in congressional elections the Democrats have done better. Representation in Congress is evenly split and the governorship is in Democratic hands. Much of the credit for the Democrats' recent success must go to former Governor Charles Robb, the late Lyndon Johnson's son-in-law. Were it not for a provision in the Virginia Constitution preventing successive gubernatorial terms, it is likely that Robb would still be governor.

WASHINGTON

Population:	4,300,000
Electoral college votes:	10
1984 election result:	Reagan 56%
	Mondale 43%

Washington in the far north-west is a mixture of wilderness and high-technology industry. It is around four hours' drive from the volcanic landscape of Mount St Helens to the headquarters of Boeing in Seattle. Like Oregon to the south, the state is a door to trade with Japan and other countries in the East and is therefore against protectionism. The electorate in this beautiful state is also concerned about the environment and its protection.

Washington is more Democratic in national races than the national average and if Dukakis performs reasonably well he should pick up the 10 electoral votes here. But Washington has not proved a good predictor of national results. In the last three close elections it has backed the loser on each occasion, supporting Nixon in 1960, Humphrey in 1968 and Ford in 1976.

WEST VIRGINIA

Population:	2,000,000
Electoral college votes:	6
1984 election result:	Reagan 55%
	Mondale 45%

West Virginia played its most significant role in a presidential election in 1960 when John F. Kennedy won the Democratic primary here, proving to the Democratic Party's bosses that a Catholic could win Protestant votes. He told audiences, 'Nobody asked me if I was a Catholic when I joined the United States Navy'. His victory over Hubert Humphrey was much assisted by the vigorous campaigning efforts of Franklin D. Roosevelt Jnr.

In presidential elections West Virginia is one of the most Democratic states. It went Democratic in all the close elections of the last 40 years and in 1980 produced Jimmy Carter's second-best result.

WISCONSIN

Population:	5,000,000
Electoral college votes:	11
1984 election results:	Reagan 54%
	Mondale 45%

Compared with the national average the Democrats have done well here in the last four presidential elections but have actually only carried the state once. Last time round it was Mondale's eighth-best result. But recently the Democrats have had good reason to worry.

In 1986 the electorate got rid of the liberal governor, Tony Earl. He was hurt by his support for gay rights. In the same year Bob Kasten, a Reaganite senator, was re-elected. Many had assumed he had made it in 1980 simply by holding on to Reagan's coat-tails and that he would be ditched in 1986. The results here this year should indicate whether there has been a real shift to the Right in the state.

Wisconsin's claim to fame in the annals of political history is as the birthplace of the Progressive movement. Robert LaFollette was elected governor in 1900 on a platform of using government power to help ordinary people. His programme, which was similar to that eventually adopted by the Democrats in the 1930s, attracted widespread support. In 1924 LaFollette gained 24% of the national vote as a presidential candidate, the best third-party result of the last 70 years.

WYOMING

Population:	600,000
Electoral college votes:	3
1984 election result:	Reagan 71%
	Mondale 28%

Wyoming has elected Democrats to the governorship for the past twenty years but in most other elections it has been a very Republican state. Its congressman and both senators are Republicans and the party has a majority in both houses of the state legislature.

This was not always so. During the New Deal it was Democratic and sent more Democrats than Republicans to Washington, as recently as 1976. But in post-war presidential elections it has produced some of the Republicans' best results.

Big government is not popular here. The electorate resents out-of-state environmentalists and federal government regulations. The government owns almost half the land in the state. Controls on the oil industry, a major employer, are energetically opposed.

CHAPTER EIGHT

Did You Know?

FACTS AND FIGURES ABOUT THE PRESIDENTS

America has been holding presidential elections for some 195 years and in all that time there have been only 39 holders of the world's most powerful office: a remarkable record of political stability in a nation noted for change.

The main political parties have also lasted well. The Democratic Party was formed by Martin Van Buren in the early 1830s (under the aegis of Andrew Jackson), while the Republican Party was founded in 1854 and won the congressional election that year.

The incumbents of the presidency, the circumstances of their arrival and departure from office, and their place in American history have long been a focus of popular interest and scholarly research. The thirty-nine presidents have kept the American publishing industry afloat for years on a raft of biographies, academic studies, political analyses and pictorial histories.

The following does not attempt to compete with any of these but represents a modest spadeful from the vast quarry of facts about the office and its holders. Anyone inspired to dig further should consult the master-miner of presidential trivia, Joseph Nathan Kane. His *Facts About the Presidents* is now in its fourth edition (he has been at it since 1959).

For beginners – a quick romp through the field.

Of the 39 presidents –
  12 were Democrats
  15 were Republicans
   1 was elected for a 4th term
   1 was elected for a 3rd term
  12 were elected for a 2nd term
   9 served full second terms

11 were elected for one term
 6 served less than one term
 9 succeeded to the presidency without election
 4 who succeeded to the presidency were subsequently elected
    in their own right
15 did not receive a majority of popular votes
 1 was impeached
 1 resigned
 7 were in their 40s when they took office
33 were over 50 when they took office
 9 were over 60 when they took office

Does it pay?

Nobody in their right mind would aim to be president for the money, but the pay is not too bad. Presidents from Washington to Grant received $25,000 a year. Since Nixon's time the president has received a salary of $200,000 (still only half what a top class baseball star might expect in a good season). He also gets a $40,000 allowance for travel and entertainment and a $50,000-a-year expense account. He travels in style, using the presidential aircraft – Air Force One, an ageing but still pretty comfortable Boeing 707, and Marine One, a powerful Sikorsky VH-3D helicopter.

Other perks include rent-free accommodation for the president and his family in the White House, a fleet of cars at his disposal, and a squad of around 25 Secret Service agents to guard him. A separate police force of over 100 guards the White House and its grounds. The president is provided with domestic servants (but must supply them with food). A yacht, belonging to the US Navy, is assigned to the president's use. He is attended by a service doctor and has access to Army and Navy hospitals.

The post carries a $82,900 pension. A former president also receives Secret Service protection for himself and his wife during his lifetime. Widows of former presidents continue to receive protection (if they want it) until their death or remarriage. A former president also receives free postal facilities, free office space, $96,000 a year for office help and, during the first thirty months after his term of office ends, up to $150,000 for staff assistance. During the first six months after their terms have ended the president and vice-president are entitled to share $1,000,000 for administrative help in winding up the affairs of their administration. The pension for a president's widow was increased in 1971 to $20,000 a year. The pension terminates if the widow remarries before the age of 60.

Next in line

If the President dies, resigns, or is removed from office, the Vice-President takes over. Next in line after the Vice-President, according to legislation passed by Congress in 1947 and 1955, are the Speaker of the House of Representatives, the President Pro-Tempore of the Senate, the Secretary of State, the Secretary of the Treasury and the Attorney-General. Fifteenth in line (allowing for the most catastrophic circumstances) is the Secretary of Education.

The measure of the man

Will the 'stature factor' be an election issue? Probably not, but here is how the candidates rank in a selection of tall and short presidents:

Abraham Lincoln	6 feet	4	inches
Lyndon B. Johnson	6 feet	3	inches
(George Bush)	**6 feet**	**2**	**inches**
Franklin D. Roosevelt	6 feet	2	inches
George Washington	6 feet	2	inches
Ronald Reagan	6 feet	1	inch
Gerald Ford	6 feet		
John F. Kennedy	6 feet		
Richard Nixon	5 feet	11½	inches
Woodrow Wilson	5 feet	11	inches
Dwight D. Eisenhower	5 feet	10½	inches
Jimmy Carter	5 feet	9½	inches
Harry Truman	5 feet	9	inches
(Michael Dukakis)	**5 feet**	**8**	**inches**
Theodore Roosevelt	5 feet	8	inches
Martin Van Buren	5 feet	6	inches
James Madison	5 feet	4	inches

First Ladies

Thirty-eight of the thirty-nine presidents married. (James Buchanan was the only president who did not.) Five presidents remarried after the death of their first wives, and one remarried after divorce (Ronald Reagan). The term 'First Lady', used to describe the wife of the president, was not heard until 1877 when it was applied to Lucy Hayes, wife of the nineteenth president, Rutherford B. Hayes.

- Lucy Hayes would not permit liquor to be served at White House functions and earned herself the nickname 'Lemonade Lucy'.

- Abigail Adams, wife of John Adams, the second president, was thought to have too much influence over her husband. Her critics sometimes referred to her as 'Her Majesty'.

- Eleanor Roosevelt, wife of FDR, drove her own car and refused Secret Service protection. She agreed however to keep a pistol in the glove compartment.

- Frances Cleveland, wife of the twenty-second president, was only 21 years old when she married Grover Cleveland, and the youngest president's wife in the White House.

- Nancy Reagan appeared in eleven films before retiring from the screen. She and Ronald Reagan appeared together in 'Hellcats of the Navy' in 1957.

- The first widow of a president to serve in an executive capacity was Eleanor Roosevelt, who was appointed in 1945 by President Truman to the US delegation to the UN General Assembly.

- Betty Ford sometimes rated higher in the opinion polls than her husband. During the 1976 campaign bumper stickers appeared that read 'Vote For Betty's Husband!'

Oldest and youngest presidents

George Bush will be 64 at the time of the election whilst Michael Dukakis will have celebrated his 55th birthday on 3 November, just five days before the poll. If Bush wins he will be one of the oldest presidents ever. (Reagan holds the record as the oldest president inaugurated (69 years and 349 days).) Dukakis might be encouraged by the fact that the average age of presidents at inauguration or succession is 55 years 209 days.

Theodore Roosevelt was 42 years and 322 days old when he succeeded to the presidency, but the youngest president elected to office was John F. Kennedy, who was 43 years and 236 days old when he was inaugurated. Kennedy, who was the first president born in the twentieth century and would, incidentally, have been 71 this year, holds the age-reversal record for presidents. He was twenty-seven years younger than the man he replaced.

Kennedy and Lincoln

On the subject of JFK, no selection of presidential facts would be complete without the following fascinating comparison of the careers of Kennedy and Abraham Lincoln.

- Both were married in their thirties to women in their twenties.

- Lincoln won election to the US House of Representatives in 1846. Kennedy was elected to the House in 1946.

- Lincoln tried and failed to get his party's nomination for vice-president in 1856. Kennedy failed in his bid to get his party's nomination for vice-president in 1956.

– Lincoln was elected president in 1860, defeating Stephen Douglas, born in 1813. Kennedy was elected president in 1960, defeating Richard Nixon, born in 1913.

– Lincoln was younger than his vice-president, Andrew Johnson, a southerner, born in 1808. Kennedy was younger than his vice-president, Lyndon B. Johnson, a southerner, born in 1908.

– Lincoln was shot on a Friday (14 April 1865) as he sat next to his wife. Kennedy was shot on a Friday (22 November 1963) as he sat next to his wife.

– Lincoln's assassin, John Wilkes Booth, fled and was killed before he could be brought to trial. Kennedy's assassin, Lee Harvey Oswald, fled and was killed before he could be brought to trial.

The twenty-year jinx

Both Lincoln and Kennedy feature in another, rather chilling, set of statistics. Beginning in 1840 and extending for well over a century, every president elected in a year ending in a zero died in office.

– William Henry Harrison, the ninth president, was elected in 1840. He caught a cold at his inauguration and died of pneumonia on 4 April 1841.

– Abraham Lincoln, the sixteenth president, was elected in 1860 and assassinated on Good Friday, 14 April 1865.

– James A. Garfield, the twentieth president, elected in 1880, was shot on 2 July 1881 and died three months later of blood poisoning.

– William McKinley, the twenty-fifth president, elected in 1900, was shot on 6 September 1901, and died a week later.

– Warren Harding, the twenty-ninth president, elected in 1920, died of a heart attack in August 1923.

– Franklin D. Roosevelt, the thirty-second president, elected in 1940 for a third term, died of natural causes some four months after taking the oath of office for a fourth term.

– John F. Kennedy, the thirty-fifth president, elected in 1960, was assassinated in Dallas, Texas on 22 November 1963.

Ronald Reagan, elected in 1980, may have broken the jinx. On 30 March 1981 President Reagan was shot in the chest by John Hinckley Jr, who fired six bullets at the President's party. Prompt medical action saved the President's life and he returned to the White House from hospital on 11 April.

Assassinations and attempted assassinations

Sadly, violence has loomed large in lives of the presidents. In addition to the four presidents murdered whilst in office – Lincoln, Garfield, McKinley and Kennedy – attempts were made against the lives of Presidents Jackson, Truman, Ford (twice) and Reagan. Assassination attempts were also made against Lincoln and Franklin D. Roosevelt when they were presidents-elect, and against former President Theodore Roosevelt when he was campaigning for re-election in 1912.

Despite this record it was only in 1965 that Congress enacted a law making it a federal crime to kill, kidnap or assault the President, Vice-President or President-elect.

Presidential firsts

George Washington was the first president whose likeness appeared on a US postage stamp – issued in 1847.

John Adams, who followed Washington in office, was the first president to live in the White House. Adams and his wife moved in on 1 November 1800. (The White House was under construction during Washington's administration.)

Thomas Jefferson was the first president to be inaugurated in Washington, DC (on 4 March 1801). John Adams, who preceded Jefferson, took the oath of office in Philadelphia. George Washington, Adams' predecessor, was inaugurated in New York for his first term, and Philadelphia for his second.

The first president to ride on a steamship (the *Savannah*) was James Monroe. The date was 1819.

Andrew Jackson, born on 15 March 1767, was the first president to be born in a log cabin.

Martin Van Buren, born on 5 December 1782, was the first president to be born a citizen of the United States. Previous presidents had been born before the American Revolution, and thus were born British subjects.

James Madison, who served from 1809–17, was the first president regularly to wear long trousers instead of knee breeches.

William Henry Harrison, the ninth president, was the first to die in office. When he died (on 4 April 1841), he had been president for only 32 days.

John Tyler was the first president to marry while in office. He married Julia Gardner in New York City on 26 June 1844.

Abraham Lincoln was the first president to be born outside the borders of the thirteen original states. Lincoln was born in Hodgenville, Kentucky, on 12 February 1809.

The first president to visit the West Coast was Rutherford B. Hayes. He arrived in San Francisco during September 1880.

James Garfield, the twentieth president, was the first left-handed president (Gerald Ford was the only other).

In 1909, William Howard Taft, the twenty-seventh president, was the first to have a car at the White House.

The first President of the United States to visit Europe was Woodrow Wilson. He sailed for France, on 4 December 1918, to negotiate the Treaty of Versailles ending the First World War.

Herbert Hoover, born in West Branch, Iowa, on 10 August 1874, was the first president born west of the Mississippi River.

Franklin D. Roosevelt was the first president elected to a third term (in 1940). He was also elected to a fourth term in 1944. Later, in 1951, the 22nd Amendment to the Constitution was adopted, limiting presidential service to two terms.

FDR was also the first president to appear on television. NBC transmitted his speech opening the New York World's Fair on 30 April 1939.

Dwight D. Eisenhower was the first president of all fifty states. Hawaii, the fiftieth state, entered the Union on 21 August 1959, during Eisenhower's second term.

John F. Kennedy, born on 29 May 1917, was the first president born in the twentieth century. He was also the first Roman Catholic elected president.

Lyndon Johnson was the first president to be sworn in by a woman. Johnson took the oath of office on 22 November 1963, following the assassination of John F. Kennedy. The oath was given by Sarah Hughes, a Federal District Judge, in the presidential aircraft Air Force One, at Love Field, Dallas, Texas.

Richard Nixon was the first president to visit all fifty states.

Nixon was also the first president to resign (on 9 August 1974).

Presidents born British subjects
Eight presidents were British subjects even though they were born in North America: Washington, John Adams, Jefferson, Madison, Monroe, John Quincy Adams, Jackson, and William Henry Harrison. The first president not born a British subject was Van Buren.

Three presidents in one year

Twice in American history there have been three presidents in one year.

- Martin Van Buren completed his four-year term on 3 March 1841. On 4 March 1841, William Henry Harrison was inaugurated. Harrison died on 4 April 1841, and on 6 April 1841, John Tyler was inaugurated president, the third president in one year.

- It happened again in 1881 when Rutherford Birchard Hayes concluded his term on 3 March 1881. On 4 March 1881, James Abram Garfield was inaugurated president. Garfield died on 19 September 1881, on which date Chester Alan Arthur, his vice-president, became president.

Occupations of the presidents

Twenty-five of the thirty-nine presidents were admitted to the Bar as attorneys, having fulfilled the legal requirements. However, they were not all graduates of law schools. The fourteen presidents not lawyers were Washington and William Henry Harrison, who were farmers and soldiers; Hoover, an engineer; Taylor, Grant and Eisenhower, professional soldiers; Andrew Johnson, Theodore Roosevelt, Harding, Truman, Kennedy, Lyndon Baines Johnson, Carter, and Reagan, elected officials. Theodore Roosevelt and Harding took courses in law but did not become lawyers.

Political experience

Presidents who had not revealed administrative ability prior to election or proved their vote-getting power were those famed for their military exploits, namely Washington, Grant and Eisenhower. Grant, however, had served in Andrew Johnson's cabinet as secretary of war ad interim.

The following is a list of the various capacities in which presidents served and of the number of presidents who served in each (some in more than one capacity):

Mayors of home towns	3
Ministers to foreign countries	7
Governors of states	15
Territorial governors	2
Vice-presidents	13
Members of presidential cabinets	9
US representatives	18
US senators	16
Members of both the House and Senate	10

Presidents and their vice-presidents

Three Republican presidential and vice-presidential teams have been elected twice: Eisenhower and Nixon; Nixon and Agnew; Reagan and Bush.

Two Democratic teams were elected for second terms: Wilson and Marshall; Franklin Roosevelt and Garner.

The only Republican vice-presidents elected to the presidency were Theodore Roosevelt, Coolidge, and Nixon. The only Democratic vice-presidents elected to the presidency were Van Buren, Truman, and Lyndon Baines Johnson.

The only presidential and vice-presidential teams defeated for a second term were Van Buren and Richard Mentor Johnson (D, 1840), Hoover and Curtis (R, 1932), and Carter and Mondale (D, 1980). Several other presidents were defeated for re-election, but each had a different vice-presidential running mate.

Vice-presidents elected president

A statistic of more than passing interest to George Bush is the number of vice-presidents to be elected to the presidency at the conclusion of their vice-presidential terms. The answer is that only three have managed it: John Adams, Thomas Jefferson (who served as president for two terms) and Martin Van Buren. In other words, the last time a vice-president achieved what Bush is attempting was 1836.

Most badly defeated president

Although John Quincy Adams was elected president in the end, he remains in the record books as being the most badly defeated presidential candidate ever, excluding those nominated by the minor parties. In the election of 1820 he received only one electoral vote, which was cast by an elector from New Hampshire, whilst James Monroe received 231 of the 232 electoral votes.

Forty presidents, thirty-nine men

In case you are wondering why the figures do not add up, remember Grover Cleveland. He was the twenty-second president – and also the twenty-fourth. He is the only president to have served two non-consecutive terms.

ON THE CAMPAIGN TRAIL 1988

'Coverage of American presidential candidatures in Britain is an odd mixture of the patronising and the adolescent.'

(*Edward Pearce,* The Sunday Times*, 8 May*)

'There isn't enough caffeine in the world to keep me awake for a Bush/Dukakis contest.'

(*Mark Russell – before Super Tuesday*)

Michael Dukakis

'The one bland Greek in the world and he's running for President . . . . Zorba the Clerk.'

(*Mark Russell, 28 April*)

'I feel bored to the point of wanting to throw something at hearing yet again that Dukakis is boring. Only boring, one feels, to people with a low threshold for serious ideas.'

(*Edward Pearce,* The Sunday Times*, 8 May*)

'There is a smuggling operation afoot, an attempt to sneak the liberal Dukakis past a generally conservative audience.'

(*Richard Cohen,* Washington Post*, July 1988*)

'People used to think that Dukakis was the bottom line of an eye-chart.'

(*Kitty Dukakis, Democratic Convention*)

George Bush

George Bush, speaking at the College of Southern Idaho on 6 May, described his relationship with President Reagan:

For seven and a half years I've worked alongside him, and I'm proud to be his partner. We've had triumphs, we've made mistakes, we've had sex – setbacks, we've had setbacks . . . I feel like the javelin competitor who won the toss and elected to receive.

'I can't tell you how difficult for me it has been over the past seven years, keeping my charisma in check so I don't upstage Ronald Reagan.'

(*George Bush, 15 March 1988*)

'The last time George Bush gave a speech someone came up and drew a chalk outline around his body.'

(*Johnny Carson, May*)

'People would remember if I attended a meeting.'
(*Lloyd Bentsen, Democratic Convention, commenting on failure of cabinet members to remember whether George Bush attended crucial meetings on selling arms to Iran*)

'Poor George, he can't help it – he was born with a silver foot in his mouth.'
(*Ann Richards, Texas State Treasurer, in keynote address to Democratic Convention 18 July*)

Jesse Jackson
Jackson 'ain't never run nothing but that mouth of his.'
(*Coleman Young, Mayor of Detroit*)

'All these experts on sub-culture, underclass. I got my life degree in sub-culture. Looked down on. Rejected. Low expectations. Told you can't make it. I was born in the slum, but the slum was not born in me. And it wasn't born in you. *You* can make it.'
(*Jesse Jackson, Democratic Convention*)

'His [Dukakis's] foreparents came to America on immigrant ships. My foreparents came to America on slave ships. But whatever the original ships, we are both in the same boat tonight.'
(*Jesse Jackson, Democratic Convention*)

Pat Robertson
'If Robertson knew where the hostages were in Lebanon, how come he didn't know where Swaggart was on Saturday night?'
(*Johnny Carson*)

Women in politics
'If you give us a chance, we can perform. After all, Ginger Rogers did everything Fred Astaire did. She just did it backwards and in high heels.'
(*Ann Richards, Democratic Convention*)

When Ms Richards was asked whether she planned to run for Governor of Texas in 1990, she said: 'At my age I don't even buy green bananas.'

Appendix 1

HOW THE STATES VOTED
in Presidential Elections 1944-1984

Figures are given as percentages

	1944	1948 (a)	1952	1956	1960	1964	1968 (b)	1972	1976	1980 (c)	1984
Alabama											
Democrat	81	54	65	57	57	–	19	26	56	47	38
Republican	18	44	35	39	42	70	14	72	43	49	61
Alaska											
Democrat	–	–	–	–	49	66	43	35	36	26	30
Republican	–	–	–	–	51	34	45	58	58	54	67
Arizona											
Democrat	59	54	42	39	44	50	35	32	40	28	33
Republican	41	44	58	61	56	50	55	65	56	61	66
Arkansas											
Democrat	70	62	56	53	50	56	30	31	65	48	38
Republican	30	21	44	46	43	43	31	69	35	48	61
California											
Democrat	57	48	43	44	50	59	45	42	48	36	41
Republican	43	47	56	54	50	41	48	55	49	53	57
Colorado											
Democrat	46	52	39	39	45	61	41	35	43	31	35
Republican	53	47	60	60	55	38	51	63	54	55	63
Connecticut											
Democrat	52	48	44	36	54	68	50	40	47	39	39
Republican	47	50	56	64	46	32	44	59	52	48	61
Delaware											
Democrat	54	49	48	45	51	61	42	39	52	45	40
Republican	45	50	52	55	49	39	45	60	47	47	60
District of Columbia											
Democrat	–	–	–	–	–	86	82	78	82	75	85
Republican	–	–	–	–	–	14	18	22	17	13	14
Florida											
Democrat	70	49	45	43	49	51	31	28	52	39	35
Republican	30	34	55	57	52	49	41	72	47	56	65
Georgia											
Democrat	82	61	70	66	63	46	27	25	67	56	40
Republican	18	18	30	33	37	54	30	75	33	41	60
Hawaii											
Democrat	–	–	–	–	50	79	60	38	51	45	44
Republican	–	–	–	–	50	21	39	63	48	43	55
Idaho											
Democrat	52	50	34	39	46	51	31	26	37	25	26
Republican	48	47	65	61	54	49	57	64	59	67	72
Illinois											
Democrat	52	50	45	40	50	60	44	41	48	42	43
Republican	48	49	55	60	50	40	47	59	50	50	56
Indiana											
Democrat	47	49	41	40	45	56	38	33	46	38	38
Republican	52	50	58	60	55	44	50	66	53	56	62
Iowa											
Democrat	48	50	36	41	43	62	41	41	49	39	46
Republican	52	48	64	59	57	38	53	58	50	51	53
Kansas											
Democrat	39	45	31	34	39	54	35	30	45	33	33
Republican	60	54	69	65	60	45	55	68	53	58	66

Figures are given as percentages

	1944	1948 (a)	1952	1956	1960	1964	1968 (b)	1972	1976	1980 (c)	1984
Kentucky											
Democrat	55	57	50	45	46	64	38	35	53	48	39
Republican	45	42	50	54	54	36	44	63	46	49	60
Louisiana											
Democrat	81	33	53	40	50	43	28	28	52	46	38
Republican	19	18	47	53	29	57	24	65	46	51	61
Maine											
Democrat	47	42	34	29	43	69	55	39	48	42	39
Republican	52	57	66	71	57	31	43	61	49	46	61
Maryland											
Democrat	52	48	44	40	54	56	44	37	53	47	47
Republican	48	49	55	60	46	34	42	61	47	44	53
Massachusetts											
Democrat	53	55	46	40	60	76	63	54	56	42	48
Republican	47	43	54	59	40	23	33	45	40	42	51
Michigan											
Democrat	50	48	44	44	51	67	48	42	46	43	40
Republican	49	49	54	56	49	33	42	56	52	49	59
Minnesota											
Democrat	52	57	44	46	51	64	54	46	55	47	50
Republican	47	40	55	54	49	36	42	52	42	43	50
Mississippi											
Democrat	94	10	60	58	36	13	23	20	50	48	37
Republican	6	3	40	25	25	87	14	78	48	49	62
Missouri											
Democrat	51	58	49	50	50	64	44	38	51	44	40
Republican	48	42	51	50	50	36	45	62	48	51	60
Montana											
Democrat	54	53	40	43	49	59	42	38	45	32	38
Republican	45	43	59	57	51	41	51	58	53	57	61
Nebraska											
Democrat	41	46	31	34	38	53	32	30	39	26	29
Republican	59	54	69	66	62	47	60	70	59	66	71
Nevada											
Democrat	55	50	39	42	51	59	39	36	46	27	32
Republican	45	47	61	58	49	41	48	64	50	63	66
New Hampshire											
Democrat	52	47	39	34	47	64	44	35	44	28	31
Republican	48	52	61	66	53	36	52	64	55	58	69
New Jersey											
Democrat	50	46	42	34	50	66	44	37	48	39	39
Republican	49	50	57	65	49	34	46	62	50	52	60
New Mexico											
Democrat	54	56	44	42	50	59	40	37	48	37	39
Republican	46	43	55	58	49	40	52	61	51	55	60
New York											
Democrat	52	45	44	38	53	69	50	41	52	44	46
Republican	47	46	56	61	47	31	44	59	48	47	54
North Carolina											
Democrat	67	58	54	51	52	56	29	29	55	47	38
Republican	33	33	46	49	48	44	40	70	44	49	62
North Dakota											
Democrat	46	43	28	38	45	63	38	36	46	26	34
Republican	54	52	71	62	55	37	56	62	52	64	65